THE KOREAN WAR

THE KOREAN WAR

THE FIGHT ACROSS THE 38TH PARALLEL

JEREMY P. MAXWELL

amber
BOOKS

© 2019 Amber Books Ltd

All rights reserved. No part of this publication may be reproduced, stored in a retrieval system, or transmitted in any form or by any means, electronic, mechanical, photocopying, recording, or otherwise, without prior written permission of the copyright holder.

Published by
Amber Books Ltd
United House
North Road
London
N7 9DP
United Kingdom
www.amberbooks.co.uk
Instagram: amberbooksltd
Facebook: www.facebook.com/amberbooks
Twitter: @amberbooks

ISBN: 978-1-78274-905-9

Project Editor: Michael Spilling
Designer: Zoe Mellors
Picture Research: Terry Forshaw

Printed in UAE

1 4 6 8 10 9 7 5 3 2

Contents

INTRODUCTION 6

1. THE UNITED STATES ENTERS THE WAR 26

2. INCHON LANDINGS 52

3. CHINESE INTERVENTION 90

4. THE WAR IN THE AIR 138

5. STALEMATE 160

6. AFTER THE ARMISTICE 190

APPENDICES 220

BIBLIOGRAPHY 220

INDEX 221

INTRODUCTION

War and imperialism did not magically commence with the outbreak of what the world has termed the Korean War in 1950. The Korean peninsula had been no stranger to foreign invaders and had had a long history of conflict with its neighbours.

CHINA, Russia and Japan all vied for influence in Korea. China and Russia shared a border with Korea, making incursions into Korea likely when each looked to flex its imperial might. The more recent attempts came from Japan towards the end of the nineteenth century, as it looked to assume its perceived place as the first modern great power in Asia. Using a major peasant rebellion in Korea against the Chinese, Japan instigated a war with China in 1894 and defeated it a year later. After another decade of imperial rivalry, Japan realized that vision when it dealt a resounding defeat to Tsarist Russian forces in the Russo–Japanese war of 1904–1905. This simultaneously stunned the world and caught the eye of US President Theodore Roosevelt, who was fascinated by the fact that a 'yellow' country had defeated a 'white' one. This also marked the beginning of the Japanese protectorate of Korea in 1905, and colony in 1910.

JAPANESE DOMINATION

The Korean people suffered under a Japanese system that sought to replace their language and change their religion. For the first

Opposite: Long trek southward, 8 January 1951: a seemingly endless file of Korean refugees slogs through snow outside of Kangnung, blocking withdrawal of ROK I Corps.

ten years, Japan ruled directly through the military, and any Korean dissent was ruthlessly crushed. After a nationwide protest against Japanese colonialism that began on 1 March 1919, Japanese rule relaxed somewhat, allowing a limited degree of freedom of expression for Koreans.

While Japanese control did benefit Korea in terms of industrialization and modernization, the Korean people suffered, especially in wartime mobilization for World War II. They were forced to work in Japanese factories and were sent as soldiers to the front. Tens of thousands of young Korean women were forced to become 'Comfort Women', effectively sexual slaves for Japanese soldiers. The Japanese also pressured Koreans to change their names to Japanese ones – an edict with which nearly 80 per cent of Koreans complied. The Koreans had to endure life under the subjugation of the Japanese until the Allies defeated them at the close of World War II.

In November 1943, the United States, Great Britain and China issued the Cairo Declaration, setting goals for the postwar order. In it, they pledged to continue the war against Japan and to

Below: The 'Big Three' – Soviet premier Joseph Stalin, US President Franklin Delano Roosevelt and British Prime Minister Winston Churchill – meet at the Tehran Conference in 1943 to discuss an Allied entry to the war on the western front.

eject Japanese forces from all the territories they had conquered, including the Chinese territories, Korea and the Pacific Islands. US President Franklin Delano Roosevelt (FDR) looked to change the existing practices in Europe and Asia with representative democracy, aid to the oppressed, free trade and open markets. It was the foundation of his vision on decolonization in the postwar period.

Realizing that previous colonies could not simply be granted complete autonomy, FDR proposed a period of trusteeship for Korea that would entail the Allied powers overseeing internal affairs while preparing Korea for independence and self-rule. At the Tehran Conference the following month, Soviet Premier Joseph Stalin expressed interest in the programme but added that the period of trusteeship should be as short as possible.

> WHILE JAPANESE CONTROL DID BENEFIT KOREA IN TERMS OF INDUSTRIALIZATION AND MODERNIZATION, THE KOREAN PEOPLE SUFFERED.

POSTWAR ORDER

While early discussion signalled a positive outcome for changes in the postwar period, FDR's plan did not clearly define how a joint trusteeship in Korea would work. More importantly, theoretical discussion, while important in establishing common goals, always depended on a Japanese surrender. At the Yalta conference in February 1945, FDR and Stalin agreed that the United States would attack the Japanese mainland while the Soviets would liberate Korea. The deal centred on the premise that the Soviets would invade Manchuria (controlled by the Japanese) at the earliest possible date following the surrender of Germany.

Such a deal came at a price. FDR and Gen. Douglas MacArthur, the Supreme Commander for the Allied Powers (SCAP), reckoned that Stalin would demand control of Manchuria, Korea and potentially parts of northern China. In a secret deal with Stalin, without the knowledge of Churchill or the Chinese leader Chiang Kai-shek, FDR conceded the Kuril Islands, the southern half of Sakhalin and special privileges in Manchuria for Soviet entry into the war against Japan. However, alliances are not easy to maintain, and the US–Soviet relationship was strained in the following months.

In July 1945, US President Harry Truman, British Prime Minister Winston Churchill and Stalin met in Potsdam to negotiate terms for the end of World War II. FDR had died three months earlier, and his death presented foreseeable problems in maintaining Allied relations. FDR had brokered all of the deals with Great Britain, China and the Soviet Union throughout the war. His successor would have to jump right in to maintain those relationships and continue with the plans for postwar order. More important than any previous agreements between FDR and Stalin, the success of the US atomic bomb presented complications that strained the relationship between the US and the Soviet Union.

> TERRITORIAL SEIZURE NOW BECAME A CLEAR ISSUE BETWEEN THE ALLIED NATIONS AND KOREA, WHICH SUDDENLY BECAME IMPORTANT TO THE UNITED STATES.

At the conference, Secretary of War Henry Stimson informed Truman that the atomic bomb would be ready for use against Japan in mere days. Having the bomb at his disposal changed matters. Truman consulted with Churchill on whether to tell Stalin. They feared that by telling him about the existence of the bomb, Stalin would try to enter the war against Japan as early as possible. With the bomb, Truman no longer needed Stalin to prosecute the attack in Manchuria and Korea that he had brokered with FDR.

Truman waited until the last possible moment to inform Stalin about the bomb. When he did, he described it in vague terms as 'an entirely novel form of a bomb'. Stalin, however, had known about the bomb for some time, and was angered by the lack of trust the Americans had shown towards the Soviet Union. He informed Truman at the conference that Soviet forces would be ready for action in mid-August. Now, with the atomic bomb no longer in development but a real tactical option, Stalin chose to advance his attack.

On 8 August 1945, two days after the first atomic bomb had been dropped on Hiroshima, the Soviet Union declared war on

Japan and invaded Manchuria a day later. Japan's surrender came a week later, after the second atomic bomb had been dropped on Nagasaki. The Soviet Union had participated in the war against Japan for only a week, but it could now reclaim the territory it had lost in the Russo–Japanese War. Territorial seizure now became a clear issue between the Allied nations and Korea, which suddenly became important to the United States.

The Soviet advance through Manchuria was so fast that it was able to occupy the Korean Peninsula before the Americans could arrive. US leaders realized that a discussion of joint trusteeship would be pointless if the Soviets already occupied all of Korea. Their solution was to approach the Soviets with a proposal to divide the peninsula into American and Soviet occupation zones, with the goal of creating a unified Korea under joint American and Soviet guidance. To make the deal, however, the US would have to decide where to divide the country.

One of those charged with making the decision was Dean Rusk, the future secretary of state under John F. Kennedy. His colleague, Lt. Gen. John E. Hull (then Chief of Operations Division), and he chose the 38th Parallel as the dividing line. Drawing the line there would ensure the US was in control of two major ports: Inchon and Pusan. Rusk would later claim that 'the 38th Parallel was recommended despite it being further north than could be reached if the Soviets did not agree to the arrangement'.

To the surprise of the US leadership, Stalin agreed to the deal. Stalin had never had grand designs for Korea. His main

Above: The remnants of Nagasaki after a plutonium implosion bomb was dropped by a B-29 on 9 August 1945, three days after the atomic bomb was dropped on the city of Hiroshima.

concern was the elimination of Japanese political and economic influence in the region. If Japanese influence persisted, it would always present a threat to Soviet interests, and Stalin was focused on regaining the position that the Soviet Union had lost in the Russo–Japanese War. He was happy to have help from the Americans.

BUILDING A NEW KOREA

On 15 August 1945, Japanese Emperor Michinomiya Hirohito announced that Japan had lost the war and would unconditionally surrender to the Allied powers. In Korea, the news brought mixed feelings. On the one hand, the Korean people rejoiced that they were finally free of Japanese control. On the other, Korea had not been liberated by its own people. As such, it would still be under the control of an outside power – the Allies, who assumed control after the Japanese surrender.

Below: Japanese signatories arrive aboard the USS *Missouri* in Tokyo Bay, 2 September 1945, to participate in surrender ceremonies.

The path for the many thousands of Japanese living in Korea was clear: they clamoured to board trains and ferries to leave Korea and return to Japan. For the Soviet Union and the United States, feelings towards Korea were not as readily apparent. Neither had thought much of Korea until the other had expressed an interest in it.

Koreans had aspired to independence from the Japanese prior to the war. However, there had never been a national figure behind whom the entire country could rally, 'so Korean claimants for power had to invent themselves as great national heroes – or allow foreign patrons to perform this service.' (Millett, A.R.: 1995.)

After the defeat of Japan, the two Korean revolutionary movements raced home from exile and established two competing 'people's wars' or 'wars of national liberation'. Thus, the civil war in Korea that began after the Japanese surrender pitted right-wing revolutionary groups, who were more numerous, with communists who were fewer in number but better organized.

Expatriate Koreans in Japan rushed home – more than a million to southern Korea and an estimated 350,000 to northern Korea – to find a disrupted economy, a swollen and underemployed population and a volatile political environment. Escaping the Russian armies sent to occupy Korea above the 38th Parallel, another million Koreans fled Manchuria and northern Korea. 'Politicians sought some sort of government that would serve revolutionary goals: (1) to end all forms of foreign domination, especially the economic and cultural oppression of Japan; (2) to create a constitutional republic that would be a single Korean nation; (3) to establish economic policies that would increase wealth, establish higher agricultural production, improve internal communications by rail and road, and create a balance between industry, extractive enterprises, and agriculture; (4) to spur a Korean version of western modernization that would not sacrifice communal values and would promote some more equitable distribution of wealth and power; and (5) to win international recognition and economic assistance.' (See Millett, A.R.: 1995.)

Above: Korean citizens watching Japanese soldiers marching towards southern ports, where they would be transported back to Japan.

ALLIED OCCUPATION

Korea's first goal was to present some semblance of a united front in the face of its occupiers. Its aims mirrored what Stalin had claimed at the Tehran Conference: that any occupation period should be as short as possible. The Japanese governor-general, the remaining symbol of Japanese rule in Korea, frantically sought free passage home and to retain some leverage over the Korean economic system. He turned power over to Yo Un-hyung (1886–1947), a well-known nationalist and leftist reformer, to form an interim government. Yo accepted this responsibility, with the provision that the Japanese release all political prisoners, on 15 August 1945, the day now recognized as Liberation Day in Korea.

The decision of Allied leaders to occupy Korea caused Yo and the Korean people great concern. The vague reference to a system by which control would eventually be transferred to Korea was not enough to calm the nerves of a country that had suffered under Japanese occupation. 'Yo transformed his emergency Committee for the Preparation of National Reconstruction into a Korean People's Republic on 6 September 1945 with most power in the hands of People's Committees at the city and county level.' (Millett, A.R.: 2005.)

Their immediate goals included measures to preserve some public order and to start a reform programme of replacing all Japanese collaborators, nationalizing Japanese property and passing laws that advanced women and the underclasses. The problem with realizing those goals was that Korean leaders still believed that the best route forward was a Korea guided by a wide range of revolutionaries.

> ITS AIMS MIRRORED WHAT STALIN HAD CLAIMED AT THE TEHRAN CONFERENCE: THAT ANY OCCUPATION PERIOD SHOULD BE AS SHORT AS POSSIBLE.

The 'central committee' that made such decisions was largely determined by three leftist revolutionaries, Yo Un-hyung, Ho Hon and Pak Hon-yong, all of whom leaned towards a socialist vision of a new Korea. On 6 September, the committee of 55 included 37 men who had some sort of socialist political orientation, including 21 members of the reborn Korean

Communist Party. Four men, including Kim Il-sung (1912–94), represented exiled communist groups. Only eight men could definitely be identified with the evangelical capitalists, six of them members or former members of the exiled Korean Provisional Government. Five men – perhaps as many as eight – eluded categorization. Twenty-five members of the committee had been political prisoners of the Japanese.

RHEE GOVERNMENT

Two days later, Yo announced a ten-man cabinet, headed by Dr Syngman Rhee. Key members of the cabinet, including Rhee, remained outside the country and would return within the following month from their respective places of exile. During that time, however, the occupying forces of the United States and the Soviet Union arrived. The US XXIV Corps, led by Lt. Gen. John R. Hodge, arrived in Seoul on 8 September; the Soviet 25th Army, led by Col. Gen. Ivan Chistiakov, occupied Pyongyang on 26 August. There were many differences in the manner in which American and Soviet forces governed their respective halves of the country. The most glaring one was that Americans became vulnerable to Korean political pressure, while the Soviets resisted any ideas that threatened their control.

As indicated earlier, the arrival of the American forces was initially well received by the South Koreans. They saw their years of bondage nearing an end. The problem in South Korea arose from the lack of American personnel who could communicate with local Korean leaders. To correct that problem, US military leaders kept Japanese people in posts and employed Japanese translators – a move that severely hindered any good will on the part of the Korean public.

Above: South Korean refugees from Taejon fleeing the advancing Red Army arrive in Taegu in July 1950 with only the possessions they can carry.

The Koreans were also not interested in any agreement that would create a unified nation and a coalition government and sought to thwart it at all costs. Southern Koreans would not accept any sort of joint US–USSR trusteeship agreement, and the Northern Koreans could not tolerate a United Nations trusteeship. 'Whatever moderate faction existed among Korean politicians disappeared through violence, repression, and intimidation on both sides of the 38th Parallel. The differences were simply too personal and too ideological for compromise.' (Millett, A.R.: 2005.)

The American response was to placate Korean leaders by progressive government and installing Korean officials in the ministries it inherited. What ensued next was a war between the competing political parties in the South. Rhee's main political rival was the Korean Independence Party leader Kim Ku, who had led the Korean Liberation Army before the end of World War II. Ku's assassins eliminated opposition from all other political parties, including two members of the Korean Democratic Party and Yo Un-hyung in 1947. Kim Ku was himself murdered in 1949 by suspects thought to be linked to the Rhee government.

In the midst of the infighting that ravaged the American-controlled territory, responsibility for policing was shared. The Korean Constabulary remained under effective American military direction. With the Korean National Police, however, the Americans maintained only an advisory role. The National Police worked quickly to suppress opposition from the South Korean Labour Party – the communists in the south.

Above: Yi Si-yeong, Vice President of South Korea (1948–51), leads cheers at the close of the UN Day ceremony in Seoul, 24 October 1950.

SYNGMAN RHEE

SYNGMAN RHEE WAS THE President of the Republic of Korea from 1948 to 1960. Born into a rural family on 26 March 1875, Rhee was a Christian convert and a zealous nationalist. In 1896, he joined the Independence Club, which consisted of a group of dedicated young men who organized protests against the Japanese and Russian empires. He spent 30 years in the United States, receiving a PhD from Princeton University and working with the Korean International Conference on measures to secure Korean independence.

Rhee returned to Korea after World War II and campaigned for the immediate independence and unification of the country. In 1948, he became the leader of the Republic of Korea and quickly purged the National Assembly members who opposed his dictatorship. He remained in power until a revolt in April 1960 unseated him. He was exiled to Hawaii, where he remained until his death in 1965.

Above: Syngman Rhee, President of the Republic of Korea, shakes hands with General Matthew B. Ridgway, Commander-in-Chief of the United Nations forces.

COMMUNIST GRIP IN THE NORTH

Consolidation north of the 38th Parallel did not drag on as long as it did in the south. On 14 October 1945, the Soviets named Kim Il-sung the secretary of the northern bureau of the Korean Communist Party. It took him less than a year to dispel opposition to his control in the north. Dedicated to Soviet-style communism, he successfully pushed communists who had fought in China to the periphery of the movement and imprisoned members of the capitalist opposition. The only real problem he faced in 1947 and 1948 was the incorporation of southern communists who had fled north.

Under the previous arrangement, the American goal was always to hand Korea back to the Korean people. In an effort to reunite the country and to thwart the tensions created by the competing ideologies forming on each side of the border, the General Assembly of the United Nations in 1947 voted to establish a nine-nation United Nations Temporary Commission on Korea (UNCOK) to be present in Korea and to supervise elections of representatives to a National Assembly that would establish a national government. The Soviet Union, however, denied the UN team entry to North Korea, effectively excluding its inhabitants from participating in the free elections. South Korea wasted little time adhering to the commission.

Six months after the UN Commission had been formed, South Korea held an election on 10 May 1948 that sent 200 representatives to the National Assembly. Three weeks later, the National Assembly held its first meeting and elected Syngman Rhee as chairman. On 15 August 1948, the government of the Republic of Korea was formally inaugurated, and the American military government in Korea was terminated. The Rhee government and Lt. Gen. Hodge (the US commander in charge) signed an interim military agreement shortly after that remained in effect until US troops were withdrawn from Korea. That withdrawal began three weeks later. By 1949, the United States recognized the new Republic of Korea.

The situation in North Korea unfolded differently. The Soviets had denied UN access, but elections within the North continued with a specific purpose. On 10 July 1948, the North

Above: Koreans cast their votes during the country's first free elections on 10 May 1948. Two hundred representatives were elected to the National Assembly and Syngman Rhee was appointed as chairman.

Korean People's Council adopted a resolution and decided on 25 August as the date for an election of members of the Supreme People's Army Assembly of Korea. The following day, the council proclaimed its control over the whole of Korea.

On 10 September, Kim Il-sung took office as the Premier of the Democratic Republic of Korea. By 25 December, the Soviet Union claimed it had removed all troops from Korea. So in the three years since the occupying forces had arrived to oust the Japanese there were two definitive Koreas, each ideologically opposed to the other and each proclaiming control over the whole country. The first phase of Korean independence ended, ushering in a new period where competition for control between the two Koreas for overall dominance ensued.

THE PATH TOWARDS WAR

With the occupying forces supposedly out of Korea, North Korea looked to promote unrest in the Republic and to replace the Rhee government with a communist one. Kim Il-sung had great visions of reunifying Korea under communist rule. Although his previous attempts to incite disorder south of the border failed to bring his vision to fruition, he had one other grand design to communize the south. In March 1949, he took his first official visit to Moscow since the formation of the Democratic Republic of Korea to obtain Stalin's approval and support to use force for reunification.

While Stalin agreed with the plan in principle, greater issues were at stake. Stalin knew that US forces were still present in Korea and that an attack would elicit a response. His decision was representative of the brewing Cold War atmosphere in which the US and the Soviet Union sought to thwart each other's control short of instigating all-out war. Kim was soured by Stalin's response, but read between the lines for Stalin's reasoning that if conditions were right, he would support his plans.

Kim continued to pursue his agenda despite the lack of aid from Stalin. On 14 October 1949, the North Korean Foreign Minister

> STALIN KNEW THAT US FORCES WERE STILL PRESENT IN KOREA AND THAT AN ATTACK WOULD ELICIT A RESPONSE.

KIM IL-SUNG

Kim Il-sung (right) was the Premier of the Democratic Republic of Korea. Born Kim Song-ju in Japanese-occupied Korea on 15 April 1912, he grew up in an environment of anti-Japanese activism. In 1920, his family went into exile in Manchuria. As a teen, he became interested in Marxism and began a career with various factions of the Chinese Communist Party. In 1935, he renamed himself Kim Il-sung. He worked his way up to a commanding role in charge of anti-Japanese activities along the Chinese–Korean border. Pushed into Siberia by the Japanese, the Soviet Army welcomed and trained him.

He fought in World War II for the Soviet Red Army, where he attained the rank of major. Kim Il-sung returned to Korea on 22 August, seven days after the Soviets accepted the Japanese surrender in the region north of the 38th Parallel that divided Korea. The Soviets appointed him head of the Provisional People's Committee. Kim immediately established the Korean People's Army (KPA), made up of veterans, and began to consolidate power in Soviet-occupied northern Korea. On 9 September 1945, Kim Il-sung announced the creation of the Democratic People's Republic of Korea, with himself as premier. He remained in power until his death on 8 July 1994.

---

sent a letter to the Secretary General of the United Nations that denied the legitimacy of UN involvement in Korea and declaring that the UN Commission would be driven out of Korea. The threat did not have the effect the Foreign Minister had hoped for. Eight days after receiving the letter, the UN General Assembly decided to continue its commission in Korea, charging it with investigating matters that might lead to military action in Korea.

As it turned out, Kim would not have to wait long for his luck with Stalin to turn. The Chinese communist forces led by

Mao Zedong defeated the Nationalist Party (Kuomintang) forces in China after a civil war that had been raging since the end of World War II. On 1 October 1949, Mao declared the creation of the People's Republic of China, and Chiang Kai-shek and his Kuomintang forces fled to the island of Formosa (Taiwan) to regroup and plan for their efforts to retake the mainland.

The fall of China to communism made matters in Korea more pressing. It was yet another indication that communism was on the rise. The US, however, maintained a hands-off policy in relation to Formosa and intended to fulfil the provisions of the Cairo Declaration that had scheduled Taiwan to be returned to China. However, Truman hesitated to completely abandon commitments to Chiang Kai-shek.

In the end, it was Britain's recognition of the People's Republic of China, Truman's neutrality with respect to the Chinese Civil War, and the US State Department's hands-off policy with respect to Taiwan that gave Stalin the impression that the US wanted to foster a relationship with China. As a result, Stalin looked to strengthen the ties between the two communist countries. When that relationship was realized with the Treaty of Friendship Alliance in February 1950, Stalin invited Kim back to discuss plans for the liberation of Korea.

While North Korea looked to both China and the Soviet Union for support in its quest to control the whole of Korea, the North Korean People's Army (NKPA) had been under the control of the Soviet Union since its inception in February 1948. The NKPA was organized under the newly established Ministry of Defence and trained exclusively by the Soviet Union. One prisoner captured late in the war claimed that, 'every training film he had ever been shown or used was made in the USSR.' Intelligence reports from the Far East Command also claimed that Premier Kim Il-sung received instructions from the Soviet Union for their Ambassador, Gen. Terenty F. Shtykov, who had commanded the Soviet occupation forces in North Korea after World War II.

Below: Mao Zedong, leader of the Chinese Communist Party, proclaims the founding of the People's Republic of China in the aftermath of his victory against Nationalist forces led by Chang Kai-shek in 1949.

Above: PRC leaders Mao Zedong and Zhou Enlai meet with Soviet Premier Joseph Stalin and Foreign Minister Andrei Vishinsky in Moscow on 14 February 1950 to sign the Treaty of Friendship, Alliance and Mutual Assistance, thereby linking the two communist nations.

By the start of the Korean War in June 1950, the NKPA was comprised of a ground force with eight infantry divisions at full strength, two more infantry divisions activated at roughly half-strength, a separate infantry regiment, a motorcycle reconnaissance regiment and an armoured brigade. Many of these contingents contained hardened veterans who had fought with Chinese communists and Soviet armies in World War II.

The North was not only developing its forces and making incursions across the 38th Parallel. The Korean Constabulary that had been formed in South Korea in January 1946 grew much more slowly than its North Korean counterpart, but by July of the following year had reached a strength of 15,000. When the Republic was established in August of that year, the constabulary became the Republic of Korea (ROK) Army. By January 1949, when the Republic was recognized by the US and the UN, the ranks of the ROK Army had swollen to more than 60,000 men. The Republic also maintained a coast guard of 4000 and a police force of 45,000.

When the last US troops left Korea in June 1949, 482 military advisors designated the Korean Military Advisor Group (KMAG) were left behind to 'advise the government of the Republic of Korea in the continued development of its security forces'. (Appleman, R.E.: 1961.) By the time the war began, ROK forces were 98,000-strong, comprising 65,000 combat troops and 33,000 headquarters and service troops. While this was an impressive organization of forces in a short period, it paled in comparison to the numerically superior and more heavily armed North Korean forces.

INVASION

Between 15 and 24 June 1950, the North Korean forces moved towards the 38th Parallel and were deployed at staging points outlined for an invasion across the border. They accomplished this as planned, without being detected by the South Korean forces or KMAG. There had been discussion of an imminent North Korean attack, but nothing was done beyond planning. American officers did not think an attack was imminent and, even if it did occur, they expected the ROK forces to thwart it. ROK forces, however, were not as confident in their ability to withstand and repulse an attack. By 24 June, the NKPA had approximately 90,000 men supported by 150 T-34 Soviet-supplied tanks waiting to attack.

> THERE HAD BEEN DISCUSSION OF AN IMMINENT NORTH KOREAN ATTACK, BUT NOTHING WAS DONE BEYOND PLANNING.

At 4.00 a.m. the following morning, North Korean forces began a coordinated attack that spanned the width of the peninsula at six locations, beginning with the Ongjin Peninsula in the west and spreading eastward from there. ROK forces and KMAG were caught completely off-guard. Many of the members of both forces were in Seoul and other towns on weekend passes. Only one regiment of the four divisions and one battalion of the separate units were in defensive positions at the parallel. They were quickly expelled by the North Korean forces and soon began to disperse when the tanks started rolling across the border.

When news of the North Korean invasion reached Washington on the evening of 24 June, many government officials, including President Truman and Secretary of State Dean Acheson, were away for the weekend. Truman had retreated to his family home in Independence, Missouri. When Acheson telephoned him with news of the invasion, he also informed him that he had requested an emergency meeting of the United Nations Security Council. During Truman's trip back to Washington, the UN Security Council voted unanimously to support an American resolution calling for the immediate cessation of hostilities and the withdrawal of North Korean troops.

Upon arriving in Washington, Truman gathered his advisors to discuss the situation. All there agreed that the Soviet Union had some involvement. Acheson recommended that Truman instruct Gen. MacArthur, Commander-in-Chief of Far East Forces, to air drop supplies, food, ammunitions and weapons to support South Korean forces. No discussion of direct US involvement occurred, however, because initial reports from Ambassador John Muccio in Korea claimed there was no need for alarm.

Muccio's cables to Washington progressively worsened, however, after North Korean successes continued to batter the ROK and KMAG defenders. Kaesong soon fell; the ancient capital city of Korea and a major trading city, this was psychologically important. The NKPA pressed forward along the main Seoul–Pyongyang highway, directly towards the capital city of Seoul. Once the North Korean attack was underway, the North Korean government declared war against South Korea in a public broadcast, claiming retaliation for a previous invasion ordered by Syngman Rhee on North Korea.

The broadcast was an attempt to justify the North Korean attack as an act of self-defence, thereby providing legitimacy for its actions. Not long after noon – roughly eight hours after the opening salvos – Premier Kim Il-sung claimed that South Korea had rejected every North Korean proposal for unification, had attacked North Korea that morning, and would have to suffer the consequences of a North Korean counter-attack. Meanwhile, American advisors had already radioed Seoul to request evacuation.

The South Korean defence continued to deteriorate quickly. Muccio's cables reflected the severity of the situation when he claimed that, 'without more ammunition, South Korean stores would be depleted in ten days'.

With rumours spreading that the NKPA was on the cusp of taking Seoul, Muccio ordered the evacuation of American civilians from Seoul. Two days after the North Koreans had crossed the border, American civilians boarded a ship from Seoul to Japan; the following day, Muccio went to Suwon, 40km (25 miles) south of Seoul. Rhee and the ROK government fled further south, to the city of Taegu. Regular Korean citizens were left helpless and on their own. Fleeing in chaos, they filled the bridges, canals and roads to escape the onslaught of the advancing NKPA forces.

Below: At a UN Security Council meeting, US delegate Warren Austin holds a Russian-made PPSh-41 submachine gun captured by American troops in July 1950. He charges that Russia is delivering arms to the North Korean regime.

1
THE UNITED STATES ENTERS THE WAR

On 28 June 1950, Seoul fell to the North Korean Army. In the aftermath of the invasion, the North Korean government and Joseph Stalin reassessed the progress that had been made. North Korean troop morale was high, but management from Pyongyang had been poor. The fall of Seoul had not spelled the end of the Rhee government.

STALIN MADE it clear to Ambassador Shtykov that he wanted the offensive to continue southward as rapidly as possible. The goal was for the North Korean People's Army (NKPA) to press forward with better efficiency and liberate the Koreans, who would then help overthrow Rhee.

While Stalin laid out his designs for Kim Il-sung to become more directly involved and sent supplies to strengthen the NKPA, the United States was awaiting word from the UN Security Council and making plans of their own to thwart the North Korean advance.

Opposite: American and KATUSA (Korean Augmentation To the United States Army) soldiers ride to the front, July 1950. Small numbers of KATUSA members were dispatched throughout the Eighth United States Army.

'FIFTH AS AN AREA OF POTENTIAL DANGER'

The day the North Koreans attacked (25 June), the US Joint Chiefs of Staff (JCS) and senior diplomats held emergency meetings to consider their options. That the attack had been a shock to the US was notable. 'The Armed Forces Security Agency responsible for ranking current threats listed Korea fifth as an area of potential danger, behind Indochina and other countries.' (Maxwell, J.P.: 2018.) In the context of the greater Cold War, it is interesting that this low assessment threat was made.

At the time, Korea was a peninsula sharing a 720-km (447-mile) border along the Manchurian province of China, and a roughly 18-km (11-mile) border with the Soviet Union by the Khasansky district of Primorsky Krai. Proximity to China and the Soviet Union alone should have suggested that Korea was a likely target. The posturing by Kim Il-sung, the premier and military leader of North Korea who had spent time fighting with the Soviet Union in World War II, should also have caused more alarm. Moreover, the Korean experience in the first half of the century with occupation, and its frequent susceptibility to foreign influence, made the Republic of Korea a likely target for the proliferation of communism.

Maj. Gen. Charles Willoughby, the G-2 (head of military intelligence) in MacArthur's Far East Command, relayed to Washington that the North Korean invasion had been 'an all-out offensive to subjugate South Korea, and that MacArthur would meet the KMAG emergency ammunition situation head on.' The JCS replied that it was considering a number of options that could be taken by the Commander-in-Chief of the Far East (MacArthur). As reports from Korea worsened, Secretary of State Dean Acheson confirmed his assessment of the situation with ambassadors posted abroad 'that the

Below: This map shows the North Korean advance from 25 June to 10 September 1950. North Korean gains were rapid, aided by the element of surprise. By 1 August, United Nations and ROK forces comprising 92,000 troops had created a defensive perimeter around the key port of Pusan.

KOREAN MILITARY ADVISORY GROUP (KMAG)

The KMAG was a United States military unit whose job it was to help train and provide logistical support for the Republic of Korea Army. In January 1946, the US military government in the south began to form a Korean defence force, and 18 lieutenants from the US Army's 40th Infantry Division were tasked with organizing eight Korean Constabulary Regiments to act as a police force. The Constabulary grew rapidly, from 2000 men in April 1946 to 50,000 in March 1948.

When the ROK declared independence on 15 August 1948, the Constabulary was absorbed into the Republic of Korea Army, and the United States created a Provisional Military Advisory Group (PMAG) to continue the work of training and advising the South Korean military. One hundred American advisors in Korea who worked under the auspices of the Department of Internal Security were reassigned to PMAG at this time, and the unit's roster was expanded. On 1 July 1949, PMAG was redesignated the United States Military Advisory Group to the Republic of Korea (KMAG). When North Korean forces invaded South Korea on 25 June 1950, KMAG became the United States Military Advisory Group, Korea, 8668th Army Unit, under the command of the Eighth United States Army.

Above: The Korean Military Assistance Group insignia includes an eagle in flight as part of the badge.

Soviets did not want a direct military conflict with the US, and that other nations would support a UN response to the invasion.'

The office of Intelligence Research also made a report on the likelihood of a ROK military collapse without American assistance. According to their report, 'the invasion was a Soviet-approved, low-risk operation to disrupt US–Japanese rapprochement and advance communism in Asia. American intervention would help hold the line in Indochina, Formosa, the Philippines, and Japan.' As Acheson's meetings continued to ponder a correct response to the situation, Army Chief of Staff Lawton Collins arrived with more ominous news of the North

Below: This soldier from the NKPA is extremely well dressed for the severe Korean winter climate. His jacket and trousers are made from thickly quilted material, the jacket featuring a doublebreasted design with zipper fastening to reduce penetration by wind chill.

Korean advance. The decision was made to get President Truman back to Washington and prepare viable options for MacArthur.

Shortly after Truman arrived in Washington, the UN Security Council responded, agreeing to a US-sponsored resolution recognizing the Republic of Korea as a 'lawfully established government', and calling for 'all members of the United Nations [to] furnish assistance to the Republic of Korea as may be necessary to repel the armed attack and restore international peace and security in the area.' Truman moved quickly, 'authorizing General MacArthur to use air and naval forces to assist the ROK in slowing the NKPA advance. He also dispatched the US Seventh Fleet to establish a blockade on Korea and defend the Formosan Straits.' (Maxwell, J.P.: 2018.) The move, while a vital beginning towards any progress in defence of the ROK, was not fast enough. The day after the forces had been dispatched, the NKPA marched into Seoul.

MacArthur hurried to assess the situation, fearing the potential threat to the entire Far East if Korea were to fall to communism. MacArthur's assessments of the situation, agreed upon by many of the senior military staff, was that only the mobilization of US Army ground forces could prevent a communist victory over Korea. From that point, common thinking suggested that it would take ground soldiers fighting an infantry war to stop the NKPA and the Chinese Communist Forces (CCF).

After the 253-man KMAG force had proven unable to defend the Han River from the NKPA, MacArthur had to find and send troops that could stand against them. The closest troops were the 24th Infantry Division of the four-division Eighth Army (1st Cavalry Division, 7th, 24th and 25th Infantry Divisions), located on Kyushu, the southernmost island of Japan. On 30 June, Gen. MacArthur instructed Gen. Walton Walker, commander of the Eighth US Army (EUSA), to order the 24th Infantry Division to Korea at once. On 1 July, Walker issued an Eighth Army Order to Maj. Gen. William Dean, commander of the 24th Infantry Division, which called on him to: (1) establish a delaying force of two rifle companies, under a battalion commander, (2) to send the division headquarters and one battalion of infantry to Pusan by air at once, (3) the remainder of the division would follow by water, and (4) to establish a base for early offensive operations. The advance elements of the landing force were ordered to 'Advance at once upon landing with delaying force, in accordance with the situation, to the north by all possible means, contact enemy now advancing south from Seoul towards Suwon and delay his advance.'

TASK FORCE SMITH HEADS NORTH

The same night that Gen. Dean was ordered to establish the delaying force, Lt. Col. Charles B. Smith, Commanding Officer, 1st Battalion, 21st Infantry Regiment, 24th Infantry Division, was awoken by his superiors and sent to Itazuke Airbase with two of his companies at once. When he arrived, Gen. Dean was waiting for him with orders. 'When you get to Pusan,' Dean said, 'head for Taejon. We want to stop the North Koreans as far from Pusan as we can. Block the main road as far north as possible.

Below: On 8 July 1950 President Truman appointed Douglas MacArthur as commander of the United Nations Command in South Korea. Here MacArthur receives the UN flag in an official presentation.

Contact General Church (KMAG). If you can't locate him, go to Taejon and beyond if you can. Sorry, that is all I can give you.'

At 8:45 a.m. on 1 July, Task Force Smith – composed of 540 men (half of a normal battalion) of the 1st Battalion, 21st Infantry Division – deployed to Korea. By 8 a.m. of the following day, Smith had landed in Pusan and made it to Taejong. After meeting with Gen. Church as ordered, Smith took a 130-km (80-mile) drive north to assess the situation near Osan. From there, he was ordered to take his men north by train to Pyeongtaek and Ansong.

While awaiting further instructions, an aerial strafing run conducted by the Royal Australian Air Force fired on the train, blowing up the train and the ammunition inside. Similar friendly fire incidents occurred at Suwon, where ROK forces and civilians fell victim to Far East Air Forces that mistook them for the enemy. On 4 July, the rest of Smith's divided command, which had followed by air and sea, arrived in Korea. That same day, a message from Gen. MacArthur to Gen. Dean stated that United States Force in Korea (USFIK) had been activated under his command, Gen. Dean assumed control of USFIK and appointed Gen. Church (KMAG) as Deputy Commander.

At midnight on 4 July, Task Force Smith moved out of Pyeongtaek for Osan, previously selected as the position where Smith would establish the delaying action against the enemy. The following morning, the 540-man force stood against approaching enemy tanks. The first wave of 33 tanks quickly penetrated through American infantry lines and then pressed through artillery positions. Ten minutes later, a second wave of North Korean tanks followed. American artillery damaged some of the tanks, but did not stop more from coming. Initially frightened, some members of the howitzer crew started to run, but regrouped once their leadership stepped in to help out.

Task Force Smith had had about an hour of silence after the tanks had passed, when Smith spotted an advancing column of

> AN AERIAL STRAFING RUN CONDUCTED BY THE ROYAL AUSTRALIAN AIR FORCE FIRED ON THE TRAIN, BLOWING UP THE TRAIN AND AMMUNITION INSIDE.

TASK FORCE SMITH

TASK FORCE SMITH WAS the first US Army ground manoeuvre unit to enter combat in Korea. On 30 June 1950, President Harry S. Truman authorized Gen. Douglas MacArthur to commit ground forces under his command to Korea. MacArthur in turn instructed Lt. Gen. Walton Walker, commander of the Eighth US Army, to order the 24th Division there. Early on 1 July, the Eighth Army provided for a makeshift infantry battalion of the 24th Division to be flown to Korea in the six C-54 transport aircraft available. The remainder of the division followed by water. The initial force was to make contact with the enemy and fight a delaying action. Task Force Smith was named for Lt. Col. Charles B. Smith, commanding officer, 1st Battalion, 21st Regiment, 24th Infantry Division, whose 540 men were the first to arrive to assist KMAG forces in Korea.

Above: Soldiers from Task Force Smith carry their equipment as they prepare to ship out to Korea. Consisting of 400 infantry with a supporting artillery battery, they were the first US troops to fight in the war at the battle of Osan on 5 July 1950.

trucks and ground troops coming towards them from Suwon. That column was the 16th and 18th Regiments of the North Korean 4th Division, a major force in the North Korean Army. The small delaying force was no match for the two units approaching. They shelled the enemy once it was within 914m (3000ft) of their position, but an estimated 1000-man infantry force rushed in, in an attempt to envelop the defending forces.

By 2.30 that afternoon, Smith looked to retreat to Osan, leapfrogging units along the ridges. The retreat, however, proved to be more deadly than the initial attack. By the next morning, Task Force Smith had lost 150 men. Survivors retreated to American lines at Pyeongtaek, Chonan, Taejon and other points in southern Korea. The initial delaying action had been a resounding defeat.

IN RETREAT

Defeat did not stop at Osan. The 34th Infantry Regiment led by Col. Jay Loveless had deployed at Pyeongtaek to catch any North Korean forces that got through Smith's forces at Osan. Fearing the same fate that befell Smith at Osan, Loveless ordered his forces to fall back from Pyeongtaek to Chonan, 13km (8 miles) to the south. Meanwhile, a battalion at Ansong fell apart to the east. Gen. Dean was furious that Pyeongtaek had been abandoned, and ordered Loveless to go back. By that time, however, it was too late: Pyeongtaek had been taken by the NKPA. Chonan fell shortly after, and US forces fled, abandoning their equipment, weapons and fellow soldiers who had died on the battlefield.

Below: A US bazooka team at Osan prepares for action as the 16th and 18th Regiments of the North Korean 4th Division advance towards them.

Above: 7 July 1950: South Korean evacuees flee south toward Taejon, the first major city south of Seoul, to escape the invading North Korean forces.

As American and ROK forces continued to retreat, MacArthur decided to commit the whole of the Eighth US Army (EUSA) to Korea. As commander of the Eighth Army, Gen. Walker visited Gen. Dean at Taejon. His command in Korea now consisted of US and remnants of the ROK forces. His immediate task was to delay the enemy advance. He established a defensive line along the south bank of the Kum River. To the east, he used the mountains and the narrow coastal corridor to delay the North Korean advance. Continued delaying actions were carried out to allow time for reinforcements to arrive from the US and the UN.

The Kum River was the first defensible river south of the Han River (border) along the route of the NKPA advance. 24km (15 miles) beyond it lay Taejon, the first major city south of Seoul along the invasion route. Dean's 24th Division was ordered to hold the Kum River line to protect Taejon. Dean's Division, however, was not able to carry out those orders. The 24th was soon overrun and the NKPA began attacking Taejon on 20 July. Dean wished to retreat as his forces became surrounded, but was ordered to hold to provide time for reinforcements to arrive from Pusan. As the NKPA surrounded and took Taejon, Dean fled to the surrounding mountains. Eventually, he became the highest-ranking American prisoner of war.

Below: The US 1st Cavalry Division land ashore on the Pohang beachhead 48km (30 miles) south of the attacking NKPA forces, in the first major amphibious operation since World War II.

While the 24th was being overrun in Taejon, the enemy 5th Division moved against Yongdok, a key point where a road led from the mountains to the coastal road. For the last half of July, UN and ROK forces battled the NKPA over Yongdok. In the push and pull between the two forces, Yongdok was taken and retaken several times. In the end, US Navy, artillery, mortar fire and air strikes facilitated the only UN victory in the region.

The two-week holding campaign at Yongdok had cost the North Korean 5th Division nearly 40 per cent of its strength in casualties. The east coast had hindered North Korean freedom of movement and aided in the effective employment of

American firepower. That type of situation did not prevail in the mountains, where the North Korean 12th Division and the ROK 8th Division fought a bitter five-day battle for control of Andong and the upper Naktong River crossing.

After the end of July, the 24th Division was in poor shape. Its members believed their trip to Korea would be a short mopping-up exercise, but the North Korean advance demonstrated that that early estimate was not accurate, and their sojourn in Korea would be long. On the major road to the west of Andong, where the North Korean 12th Division was recuperating from the battles fought in the last half of July, was the town of Sangju.

This was the crossroads for all of the mountain roads in that region of Korea. It sat south of the Mungyeong Plateau and the dividing watershed between the Han and Naktong rivers. Moreover, it was the strongest position in the valley of the Naktong, north of Taegu.

THE SEGREGATED 24TH INFANTRY

Towards the latter part of July, Eighth Army commander Gen. Walker ordered the US 25th Division to concentrate there and bolster ROK defence of the central mountain corridors. Yechon was the 25th Division's first combat engagement against the NKPA. The 25th Division was tasked with retaking Yechon after it had been lost the day before. The 3rd Battalion of the 24th Regiment, commanded by Lt. Col. Samuel Pierce, Jr., was selected for the job, and black paratrooper Bradley Briggs, commander of Company L, led the charge that took the town back from North Korean control.

Charles M. Bussey, commander of the 77th ECC that ended up spearheading the attack – although originally only tasked to

24TH INFANTRY REGIMENT

AN AFRICAN-American unit was stationed in Gifu, Japan, as part of the US occupying forces after World War II. Prior to the Korean War, it was organized as a permanent regiment of the 25th Infantry Division. Despite the desegregation of the US armed forces in 1948 by Executive Order 9981, the 24th Infantry remained predominantly African-American, with an officer corps of both African and European Americans.

In late June 1950, soon after North Korea invaded South Korea, the 24th deployed to Korea to assist in the Korean War. It fought throughout the Korean peninsula, from the defence of the 'Pusan Perimeter' to its breakout and the pursuit of communist forces well into North Korea, to the Chinese counter-offensives, and finally to UN counter-offensives that stabilized near the current Demilitarized Zone. The 24th was disbanded at the end of the war, as integration was carried out across the Far East Command.

Above: Members of the all black 24th Infantry Regiment west of Sangju on their way towards the fighting on the Pusan Perimeter.

provide support – describes the village of Yechon as 'cradled deep in a buttonhook mountain that nearly ringed and loomed above it.' Furthermore, 'the enemy had fallen back, climbed part way up the mountain, and rained fire down upon the town.' Bussey grabbed straggling soldiers and mounted a defence with a .50-calibre machine gun and ground mount, and a water-cooled .30-calibre machine gun. As the opposing forces scaled down the mountain towards their position, the 24th RCT mowed them down until there was no further resistance. Despite the heroism displayed by Bussey and members of his unit, the events at Yechon have been shrouded in controversy; so much so that the Army would later try to strike the events that transpired at Yechon from the official record.

> AS THE OPPOSING FORCES SCALED DOWN THE MOUNTAIN TOWARDS THEIR POSITION, THE 24TH RCT MOWED THEM DOWN UNTIL THERE WAS NO FURTHER RESISTANCE.

Continued hardships would also affect any prowess felt by African-Americans as a result of their first successful engagement. Six days after Yechon, near Sangju, the 24th was pushed back by North Korean forces bearing down the hill towards them. Losing ground, and shifting back as the situation dictated, members of the 24th were reported to have 'bugged out'. Although the 24th displayed heroism and fortitude in the fighting on 26 July, 'many commanders believed that race was at the root of what had happened.'

Maj. Eugene Carson, acting commander of the 1st Battalion, later told Eighth Army investigators that 'I think that when [the men of the 24th] … become scared they react with an animal instinct. …I am not saying that all the men are like that. Five or ten percent are not, but I am saying that there is about 85 or 90 percent that do react this way. …These people are different in instincts.' Carson's words, echoed by many white commanders of the 25th Division, were a shocking reminder that black soldiers would be used as scapegoats when something went wrong. The entire 25th Division and the rest of the Eighth Army forces were failing to meet the NKPA advance.

By the end of July, NKPA forces had pushed Eighth Army forces into a position known as the 'Pusan Perimeter', where they found themselves surrounded on two sides with their back facing the water. Further Army regiments, and the 1st Marine Provisional Brigade, landed at Pusan on 2 August. On 18 August, the 24th Regimental Combat Team met the North Korean 6th Division at Battle Mountain while defending the Pusan Perimeter, the area with which they had been charged. Battle Mountain was fought over beginning on 15 August and continued for the rest of the month. Charles Bussey stated that the 24th Infantry Regiment lost and regained the hill for 45 days.

> THE EIGHTH ARMY WANTED TO GO ON THE OFFENSIVE, YET THEY TOO HAD SUFFERED MANY CASUALTIES.

Each side had recognized the importance of the peak as a vantage point for repelling opposing forces. On 20 August, the NKPA 6th Division intensified their assault on the 24th Infantry Regiment. Most held their ground, but Company E buckled under the pressure. SFC Willis Blakely, the platoon leader of Company E, later claimed that only eight of his men had run, and 15 had stayed, but the die was cast for the 24th. White commanders renewed their doubts about blacks as soldiers. Due to an unwillingness to acknowledge that failures were as likely the result of unskilled white officers, the blame fell on the black infantrymen.

NAKTONG OFFENSIVE
On 31 August 1950, the 6th and 7th Divisions of the NKPA attacked US and ROK forces in the Naktong Offensive. The NKPA 'understood that Pusan was the source of American strength, [and] the enemy resolved to eliminate the threat.' (Maxwell, J.P.: 2018.) Their forces had been

severely diminished in the preceding month, and malnourishment took its toll on the remaining soldiers. They eventually fell to American artillery and air support. The Eighth Army wanted to go on the offensive, yet they too had suffered many casualties. The 25th Division had lost nearly 40 per cent of its force. While replacements started to trickle in, all regiments were still understrength.

Officers arrived in sufficient numbers, even as enlisted replacements remained substantially below what was needed. During this period, more black troops had arrived than whites, which led to their assignment to all-white units of the 25th to bring them up to strength. One of these first attempts at integration was in the 9th Infantry Regiment – one of the first contingents to land in July 1950. Col. John G. Hill, commander of the 9th Infantry Regiment, claimed that circumstances forced him to shift his excess black soldiers to white battalions. According to Hill, 'there were no replacements. We had to use untrained South Korean contingents. We would have been doing ourselves a disservice to permit [Negro] soldiers to lie around in rear areas at the expense of the still further weakening of our [white] rifle companies.'

Below: September 1950. Men of the 9th Infantry Regiment hitch a ride on an M-26 Pershing tank. They would soon be embroiled in the impending Naktong Offensive planned by the NKPA's 6th and 7th Divisions.

Above: An integrated unit, 20 November 1950. Fighting with the 2nd Infantry Division north of the Chongchon River, Sfc. Major Cleveland, weapons squad leader, points out North Korean positions to his machine gun crew.

Integration had finally arrived in the US Army: it was a beginning, however modest. Real integration would not happen until later in the war, when the demands of the conflict dictated it. The news of African-American units retreating from the enemy should not have been as big of an issue as it turned out to be. US units had fled in the face of the enemy before; Task Force Smith was a clear example. The 24th Infantry Regiment, however, was a segregated US unit, comprised mainly of African-American soldiers. In the US military, that fact alone was enough to cast doubt on their capabilities as soldiers.

Their fate in Korea was telling of the nature of race relations in the United States, and an important issue within the growing political war between the US and the Soviet Union. The United States had led the charge against communism in the wake of World War II and sought measures to combat the spread of what they deemed a repressive way of life. The fact that they maintained a segregated society did not hold up the image they had presented of themselves to the world as the arbiters of democracy and self-determination.

Soviet, Chinese and North Korean armies tried to capitalize on this by dropping psychological warfare leaflets aimed at African-Americans, asking them why they were fighting for a country that treated them as second-class citizens. It also became an important tool in prisoner-of-war camps, when NKPA forces looked to break prisoners or use the issue in the re-education process.

THE PUSAN PERIMETER

At the end of August, the Eighth Army was in a bad situation. Gen. Walker had no choice but to fight a delaying action as he tried to build up sufficient force to mount an offensive. He also had to hold Pusan, the only deep-water port in South Korea, at all costs. But by the end of July, Walker was running out of space. If he withdrew any further, he would lack sufficient depth with which to manoeuvre the reserves necessary to block enemy thrusts and eventually mass for a counter-attack and breakout.

On 29 July, Walker issued his 'Stand or Die' order to his division commanders. The severity of the situation dictated his ominous warnings. In those orders, he proclaimed:

> We are fighting a battle against time. There will be no more retreating, withdrawal or readjustment of the lines or any other term you choose. There is no line behind us to which we can retreat…. There will be no Dunkirk, there will be no Bataan. A retreat to Pusan would be one of the greatest butcheries in history. We must fight until the end…. We will

Below: A US Marine carries ammunition for his M1 .30 calibre rifle in cotton bandoliers across his chest. He is dressed in M1944 olive-drab fatigues.

fight as a team. If some of us must die, we will die fighting together.... I want everybody to understand we are going to hold this line. We are going to win.

At the time Walker issued his bold order, the forces under his command included five badly mauled ROK divisions and the still understrength US 24th and 25th Infantry Divisions and 1st Cavalry Division. As the battle progressed, reinforcements arrived through Pusan, including the 5th Regimental Combat Team (5th RCT), the 1st Marine Provisional Brigade (1st Marine Brigade), the 2nd Infantry Division and the British 27th Infantry Brigade.

By 1 August, Walker's forces had retreated beyond the Naktong River, and the Pusan Perimeter comprised a rectangle approximately 160 by 80km (100 by 50 miles) in the southeast corner of Korea. To the west, the main line of resistance ran along the Naktong, from the mountain town of Naktong-ni some 130km (80 miles) south; at the confluence with the Nam River, the Naktong cut sharply east, but the defensive line continued 32km (20 miles) due south to the coast. The northern boundary of the perimeter ran through the mountains from Naktong-ni to the town of Yongdok, on the east coast. The sea bounded the eastern and southern sides of the perimeter, and Walker could rely on US Navy fire support along the perimeter's two coastal anchor points.

Walker operated within interior lines well. The US Fifth Air Force maintained total air supremacy, which meant Walker could move forces within the perimeter during daylight hours without fear of detection. An excellent rail loop within the perimeter connected Pusan with Miryang, Taegu and P'ohang-dong. The port itself, on the Tsushima Strait, provided the means of resupplying his forces.

Walker initially positioned his three American divisions along the Naktong, from Waegwan south to the coast. The 24th Infantry Division held the centre, with the 1st Cavalry Division on the right and the 25th Infantry

Opposite: August 1950. Fresh and eager US Marines get organized at Pusan to head north to the fight. Pusan was the largest port and therefore the most vital point of entry for troops and supplies still controlled by UN and ROK forces.

Below: General Walton Walker (left), commander of the Eighth US Army (EUSA), issues orders to hold the Pusan Perimeter, July 1950.

Above: A North Korean T-34/85 medium tank. Before the outbreak of the Korean War, Joseph Stalin equipped the KPA with over 200 tanks, including Soviet T-34s, the mainstay of Soviet armoured forces throughout World War II.

Division on the left. North of the 1st Cavalry Division, the ROK 1st Division held the Naktong up to the northwest corner of the perimeter. Manning the northern flank were the ROK 6th Division in the west and the 8th and Capital Divisions in the centre. The ROK 3rd Division defended the northeast corner through Yongdok to the coast.

NORTH KOREA GOES ON THE OFFENSIVE

The North Koreans initially threw six infantry divisions against the western flank of the perimeter and four against the northern flank. The NKPA 105th Armoured Division was held in reserve. Although the 105th was armed with the highly capable Soviet T-34 tank, the unit had suffered heavy losses during its advance and was down to only about 40 operational tanks.

However, the North Koreans continued to send fresh forces down the peninsula; by late August, they were able to commit three additional divisions, two against the centre of the Naktong line and one against the southern end near the coast. Walker's force actually held a slight numerical advantage in the first weeks of August. The majority of the NPKA soldiers were combat troops, however, whereas the majority of Walker's soldiers were support troops necessary to operate the Allies' extensive logistics infrastructure.

Walker planned to conduct a 'mobile defence', where a small portion of one's defending force holds a thin screen of forward strongpoints while the bulk of the force is held in reserve as a counter-attack element. A positional defence assumed a frontage of 10–13km (6–8 miles) for each division. By contrast, each of Walker's four divisions along the Naktong had to hold fronts of 40–56km (25–35 miles). This line of strongpoints was so long and thinly spread that Walker lacked sufficient troops to form the key large mobile reserve. Thus, he was forced to cobble together a series of ad hoc counter-attack forces from troops in quiet sectors and newly arriving units, throwing them in whenever and wherever the NKPA penetrated his line. Thanks to a good network of roads and railroads within the perimeter, Walker usually managed to move his 'fire brigades' where he needed them.

> THANKS TO A GOOD NETWORK OF ROADS AND RAILROADS WITHIN THE PERIMETER, WALKER USUALLY MANAGED TO MOVE HIS 'FIRE BRIGADES' WHERE HE NEEDED THEM.

Between 5 and 24 August, the NKPA attacked the Pusan Perimeter along four widely separated but converging axes. In the southwest, one NKPA division and one armoured regiment advanced along the Chinju–Masan–Pusan axis, seeking to envelop the left of Walker's line. Walker reinforced the 25th Infantry Division with the newly arrived 5th RCT and the 1st Marine Brigade. Designated Task Force Kean, the combined Army–Marine force launched the first American counter-attack of the war on 7 August, hitting the NKPA 6th Division

Below: A US M26 Pershing tank. Used extensively throughout the Korean War, the M26 outmatched the North Korean T-34/85 in terms of firepower and protection but was challenged by the hilly and muddy terrain.

Above: A pair of disabled North Korean T-34 tanks lie in waste along the Pusan Perimeter.

at Chinju. The poorly coordinated counter-attack stopped the North Koreans, but otherwise produced limited results. After five days of indecisive fighting, Walker prudently suspended the operation. He faced more serious threats farther north.

At the same time, the North Koreans drove for the centre of Walker's line, launching five infantry divisions echeloned in depth, supported by elements of the 105th Armoured Division. This double-pincer attack originated around Sangju and sought to envelop Taegu from both the north and south. Walker considered the southern thrust, through an area dubbed the 'Naktong Bulge', the greater threat, as it endangered the vital Taegu–Pusan rail loop.

The North Korean thrusts, however, were poorly coordinated, allowing Walker to shift his reserves between the two. He brought the 1st Marine Brigade and elements of the 27th Infantry Regiment north and attached them to the 24th Infantry Division. Counter-attacking the NKPA 4th Division on 17 August, the 24th Infantry Division cleared the bulge by the following night. On 24 August, Walker put the newly arrived 2nd Infantry Division into the centre of the line and pulled the 24th Infantry Division back into reserve.

ASSAULT ON THE PERIMETER

While the North Koreans were attacking in the centre and south, two NKPA divisions north of Taegu forced their way across the Naktong and collapsed the northwest corner of the perimeter. Withdrawing south under intense pressure, the ROK 1st and 6th divisions fell back into the 1st Cavalry Division, forcing Walker to evacuate his Eighth Army headquarters from Taegu to Pusan. Walker shifted the 27th Infantry north and again counter-attacked with the ROK 1st Division.

By 18 August, the Americans and South Koreans had established defensive positions overlooking a long, flat, narrow valley that became known as the 'Bowling Alley'. The following day, Walker committed elements of the 23rd Infantry Regiment to reinforce the 27th. The battle dragged on for six more days and nights, as the NKPA 13th Division tried unsuccessfully to push the Americans back.

THIS DOUBLE-PINCER ATTACK ORIGINATED AROUND SANGJU AND SOUGHT TO ENVELOP TAEGU FROM BOTH THE NORTH AND SOUTH.

As the series of battles was raging along the Naktong, the NKPA attempted to infiltrate and envelop the northern perimeter with three divisions. The North Korean objective was to drive down the east coast, from Yongdok, through P'ohang-dong to Pusan. The northern flank was under the tactical control of the ROK I Corps, but Walker committed a small task force of US artillery and armour, and the South Koreans received air and naval support from the Far East Command.

Naval gunfire compensated for ROK 3rd Division artillery shortcomings, forcing the NKPA to operate far inland.

50 THE UNITED STATES ENTERS THE WAR

Below: A GI resting after serving 43 straight days on the front lines in Korea, September 1950. Due to understrength forces at the start of the war, enlistments were extended and troops spent long tours on the front until a limited rotation policy was established.

Regardless, the NKPA managed to push the South Koreans down the coast to Toksong-ni. The US Navy evacuated the ROK troops on the night of 16–17 August, putting them back ashore the following day to establish defensive positions near P'ohang-dong, some 40km (25 miles) further south. The 3rd Division remained in the fight, but the Pusan Perimeter had collapsed southward to little more than half its original size.

The North Korean push in early August had amounted to a massive frontal attack, but a piecemeal one. On 27 August, the NKPA launched another series of attacks against the same objectives, but this time the attacks were well coordinated. Despite heavy initial losses, they were still able to field some 98,000 troops. By 3 September, Walker was beating back simultaneous attacks in five locations.

Three days later, the North Koreans cut the key road running west to Taegu, forcing the ROK 3rd Division out of P'ohang-dong. In the centre, the North Koreans almost pushed the 1st Cavalry out of Taegu by 10 September and drove the 2nd Infantry Division back into the Naktong Bulge, almost to Yongsan.

Above: US Marines guard three captured North Koreans near Seoul, autumn 1950.

In the far south, the NKPA broke through the 25th Infantry Division and advanced towards Masan.

Walker focused squarely on the security of Pusan. His defences held on grimly, and the North Korean offensive peaked by 12 September. The NKPA still had some 70,000 effectives in the field, but they had stalled all around the Pusan Perimeter. Walker knew that his only hope for a breakout would centre on Gen. MacArthur's plan to land troops behind the enemy.

2

INCHON LANDINGS

The Pusan Perimeter was vital to the overall success of the war. MacArthur realized that he could lose the war if General Walton Walker (commander of the Eighth US Army) could not hold it. Moreover, he felt that only a major amphibious assault that would change the strategic balance was needed to accomplish that.

Proposed for 22 July 1950, objectives included striking enemy communications at Seoul and pushing them back across the 38th Parallel. The plan was scrapped, however, because US and ROK forces were unable to stop the North Korean drive southward. That did not stop MacArthur from continuing his grand plan for an amphibious landing. He ordered the Joint Strategic Plans and Operations Group (JSPOG) to continue planning the assault, and on 23 July they announced Operation Chromite.

AMPHIBIOUS LANDING

Operation Chromite called for an amphibious landing in September and proposed three plans. The first called for a

Opposite: US troops descend down ropes to landing crafts for the amphibious landing on Inchon. The Inchon landing was General MacArthur's grand plan to turn the tide of the war.

landing at Inchon on the west coast. The second called for a landing at Kunsan on the west coast. The final plan proposed a landing at Chuminjin-up on the east coast. MacArthur favoured the plan to land at Inchon. He scheduled the operation for mid-September, with the 5th Marines and the 2nd Infantry Division landing behind the enemy amid a simultaneous attack by the Eighth Army. Unfortunately for him, the North Korean forces continued to press forward against the defending US and ROK forces.

Since the Eighth Army was providing the main defence of the Pusan Perimeter, the US 2nd Infantry Division and the 1st Provisional Marine Brigade were tasked to join them in their efforts. Faced with the threat of his plans being unrealized, MacArthur decided to commit his only reserve forces in Japan, the 7th Infantry Division, once it could be brought up to combat strength.

MacArthur stayed very close to the development of the Inchon landing. He understood what his planners were considering. Even before he sent word to the Department of the Army about his plan to land behind the enemy, he had already decided on it. He moved quickly, establishing a Special Panning Staff comprised of members of his Far East Command Staff. On 21 August, he requested authority from the Department of the Army to activate X Corps, the force he would use to prosecute his amphibious

Below: General Douglas MacArthur (second from left), Commander-in-Chief of Far East and UN Forces, Army Chief-of-Staff J. Lawton Collins (left), Chief of Naval Operations Admiral Forest Sherman (second from right), and Admiral Arthur William Radford (right), Commander-in-Chief of the Pacific Command (CINCPAC), plan the Inchon Landing, August 1950.

landing at Inchon. Five days later, with approval in hand, he activated the corps and designated that all units then residing in Japan or on their way to the Far East Command be assigned to GHQ Reserve and assigned to X Corps.

As commander of X Corps, MacArthur chose his Chief of Staff, Gen. Edward (Ned) Almond. While Almond was exacting and expected great dedication from those who served under him, his lacklustre performance as commander of the 92nd Division in Italy during World War II begged the question why MacArthur placed so much trust in his ability to command such a large-scale operation. MacArthur never entertained the idea that the landing could fail, however, and remained under the impression that not only would it be a success, but also that North Korean forces would be routed, Seoul retaken and the war end shortly after that.

That belief in assured success drove MacArthur's decision to make Almond commander of X Corps while simultaneously retaining his job as Chief of Staff of the Far East Command. That decision led to division among many of the corps commanders in Korea because it placed Almond in roles that defied the normal chain of command, such as in his dealings with superior staff such as Gen. Walton Walker, who commanded the Eighth Army forces that were meant to link up with X Corps.

Above: August 1950 – halftracks, trucks and tanks swarming ashore from ships at Pusan docks, the main port of entry for US and UN personnel in the Republic of Korea.

OPERATION CHROMITE

THE AMPHIBIOUS ASSAULT TOOK place behind North Korean lines at Inchon, a port city on South Korea's west coast close to Seoul and North Korean Army supply lines. Planned by Gen. MacArthur and carried out by X Corps, its objectives were fourfold: to neutralize the fortified Wolmi Island, which controlled access to Inchon Harbour; to land and capture Inchon, 40km (25 miles) west of Seoul; to seize Kimpo Airfield just south of Seoul; and finally to capture the city of Seoul. As part of his overall plan, Gen. MacArthur envisioned that the Eighth US Army would break out of the Pusan Perimeter at the same time as the Inchon landing and push the North Korean Army northwards, trapping it between the two forces.

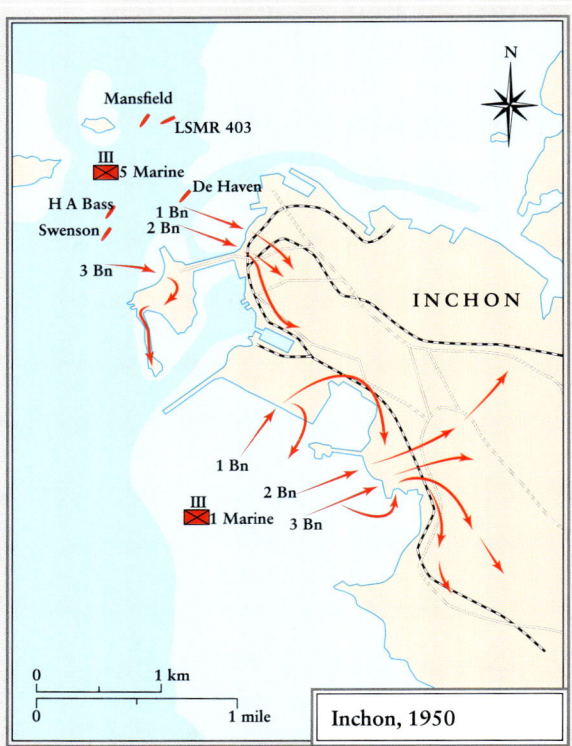

Inchon, 1950

PLANNING PROBLEMS

Chain-of-command issues were not the only problem. The planning phases of the Inchon landing were mired with problems from the activation of X Corps. For starters, when MacArthur received authorization from the Department of the Army for a landing behind enemy lines, he failed to mention that he had settled on Inchon as the location. The location of Inchon itself became a divisive issue between Almond, his Deputy Chief of Staff, members of the JSPOG who supported the location, and Gen. Lawton Collins (the Army Chief of Staff) and senior staff of the Navy and Marine Corps. While at this stage more of a trumpet for the expressed wishes of MacArthur, Almond found himself frequently at odds with his cohorts, particularly

Maj. Gen. Oliver P. Smith, commander of the 1st Marine Division, which made up one of the major ground units of X Corps.

The Navy's concern was the difficult tides that existed at Inchon Harbour, which reached heights of 9m (30ft). If the ships and landing craft did not offload personnel and supplies in time, they could be stranded resting atop the floor of the harbour, sitting ducks to enemy attack. Moreover, the Marines were tasked with assaulting Wolmido Island, a tiny island reinforced with enemy artillery that stood in the way of ships en route to the harbour. Landing at Inchon demanded that Wolmido be taken first.

The tides, current and the winding Flying Fish Channel that lacked significant depth exposed opposing forces to point-blank fire from its defenders. Fears remained that only small ships such as destroyers could traverse the channel; on their arrival, they would be forced to anchor because the current would otherwise dash them into the mud. Also, if they anchored, the destroyers automatically gave up their prime advantages of speed and manoeuvrability and would be vulnerable to the guns atop Wolmido.

Despite the arguments made by the Navy and Marine Corps, who, based on the scope and purpose of their mandates, had more experience with amphibious landings, MacArthur continued with his plans. Instead of giving way to caution, he

Above: US troops rest on a pier after disembarking from a ship somewhere in Korea, August 1950.

Above: 15 September 1950: US Marines use scaling ladders to carry out their amphibious assault on Inchon.

argued that the very reasons his opponents had proposed against it made it necessary. Moreover, he reasoned that an assault on Inchon was necessary because 'the enemy had neglected his rear and was dangling on a thin logistical rope that could be cut in the Seoul area, that the enemy had committed practically all of its forces against the Eighth Army in the south and had no trained reserves and little power of recuperation.'

Inchon, MacArthur claimed, was strategically necessary to secure the quick recapture of the South Korean capital of Seoul. Such a manoeuvre, he posited to his detractors, 'would hold the imagination of Asia and win support for the United Nations.' The more that the Joint Chiefs of Staff and Lawton Collins pressured MacArthur to change the site of the landing, the more he dug in. Inchon was the place and Operation Chromite would begin on 15 September.

When the lead elements of Operation Chromite loaded out from Japan, a typhoon threatened the port of Kobe, where 50 vessels were assembled. For three days, MacArthur, X Corps leaders and onlookers from Washington wondered if Chromite would be able to meet its 11 September date for disembarkment. Despite damages inflicted by the typhoon on the port of Kobe, the 1st Marine Division left on 11 September to converge with 7th Division, which left for Yokohama, and the 5th Marines, which left Pusan.

Aerial bombardment to isolate the designated invasion had begun prior to the invasion forces landing on 4 September. On 10 September, Marine air elements deployed napalm over Wolmido to neutralize the enemy coastal batteries. The inner harbour of Inchon was also attacked by a Gunfire Support Group comprised of two US heavy cruisers, two British light cruisers and six US destroyers from 13 September until two days later, when the X Corps expeditionary troops arrived.

US and South Korean Marines, along with their counterparts from Australia, Canada, France, the Netherlands, New Zealand and the United Kingdom, launched the landing in three separate locations. Lead elements of 10th Corps hit 'Green Beach' on the north side of Wolmido Island. Its landing force consisted of 3rd Battalion, 5th Marines and nine M26 Pershing tanks from the 1st Tank Battalion. Meanwhile, Combat Team 5, which included 3rd Battalion South Korean Marines, scaled the seawalls along 'Red Beach'.

Within 24 hours of the main landing, the 1st Marine Division had overpowered the North Korean defences and opened the causeway that enabled tanks from Green Beach to enter the fight.

Below: Brigadier General Courtney Whitney (left), General Douglas MacArthur (centre), and Major General Edward Almond (at right, pointing), commander of X Corps, observe the shelling of Inchon from the USS *Mount McKinley*.

To the south, the 1st Marine Regiment arrived at 'Blue Beach', where they encountered little resistance because North Korean forces had already surrendered.

RECAPTURING SEOUL

With the Inchon landing a success, UN forces had to finish the job by routing the enemy at Seoul, the South Korean capital that had been abandoned by its government in the face of the North Korean onslaught. To retake Seoul, UN forces would have to cross the Han River, a natural barrier standing between

them and defending North Korean Forces. After sending out a reconnaissance company to assess the possibility of using amphibious LVTs (Landing Vehicle, Tracked) for the crossing, Company I of the US 5th Marines began the assault at 6.45 a.m. on 20 September. Meeting little resistance thanks to the heavy artillery bombardment laid out in preparation for the crossing, the Marines moved to cut off the Seoul–Kaesong railroad and follow it to Seoul. When night descended on the first day, the 5th Marines and the 2nd Battalion, ROK Marines were across the river and had begun setting up a pontoon ferry at the crossing site. The relatively easy crossing, however, would not be indicative of the North Korean resolve.

Below: 15 September 1950: Landing Ship Tanks (LSTs) unload men and equipment on a beach during the Inchon landings. Three of the LSTs shown are LST-611, LST-745 and LST-715.

Above: 26 September 1950: a US Marine M26 tank follows a line of prisoners-of-war down a village street after the capture of Seoul.

The following morning, the Marines were met with steadily growing resistance. Fighting through a company-sized counter-attack and through 8km (5 miles) of terrain along the Han River, they managed to make it all the way to within 5km (3 miles) of the mail railway station in Seoul. Their success prompted Gen. MacArthur to return to Tokyo, feeling that the situation was in hand and that the capture of Seoul would soon be realized. Little did anyone realize at that point that the 5th Marines would be held at that position through four days of intense battle, as North Korean forces had chosen that location – the western approach to Seoul – as its main line of defence.

While the 5th Marines were fighting for Yongdungpo, the industrial suburb on the south bank of the Han River, the 7th Marines – the third regiment of the 1st Marine Division – arrived in Inchon Harbour and began unloading. With close to 50,000 soldiers, more than 5000 vehicles and over 20,000 tons of cargo ashore in Korea, command for the Inchon operation transferred from Admiral Arthur Struble, who was commander of the US 7th Fleet and responsible for the landing, to Gen. Almond, who assumed command of the Seoul operation as commander of X Corps.

With Yondungpo secure, the 1st Marine Division ordered the operation to capture Seoul. According to its plan, the 1st Marines would cross the Han at Yongdungpo and join the 5th Marines north of the river. The 7th Marines would then move up from Inchon and establish a three-regiment line. Initially, the capture of Seoul was to be accomplished by a completely Marine ground force. At the last minute, however, Gen. Almond altered the plan, indicating that the ROK Marines and the ROK 17th Regiment were also to be used to secure the city. That move by Almond was one of many attempts to exert his control over 1st Marine Division commanders.

The Marines made great progress, but the fighting in the western section of Seoul was intense. At one point on 23 September, Gen. Almond instructed 1st Marine Division commander Maj. Gen. Oliver P. Smith that if progress were not made, he would change the division boundaries. Doing just that, Almond called a commanders' meeting to change the boundaries between the 1st Marine Division and the 7th Infantry Division. He also ordered the 32nd Regiment, with the help of the ROK 17th Regiment attached, to attack the Han River into Seoul the next morning. Fighting through the hills that lined the western entry and the barricades in place remained intense, and only proved successful with artillery and armoured support.

> FIGHTING THROUGH THE HILLS THAT LINED THE WESTERN ENTRY AND THE BARRICADES IN PLACE REMAINED INTENSE.

On 25 September, the Marines were inside Seoul and the 7th Division held the South Mountain. The fighting on the western edges of the city remained intense. With the help of the 32nd Division and the ROK 17th Regiment, the 1st Marine Division entered Seoul on 25 September. In a hasty declaration, probably to satisfy the wishes of Gen. MacArthur, Gen. Almond announced the liberation of Seoul. At the time, less than half of Seoul was secure. While fighting between barricades was still raging with North Korean forces that had been ordered to stay behind in a last stand, MacArthur issued UN Command Communiqué No. 9 stating that Seoul had been recaptured.

THE UN COALITION

While the Inchon landing was a necessary step in turning the tide of the war, it marked the shift from a wholly US-led resistance to a collaborative UN effort. Founded in 1945, the United Nations was formed with 51 originating members. At the outbreak of the Korean War, there were 59 member nations; 48 either sent forces or aid to Korea or offered to.

Of the member nations, 16 countries sent combat troops to South Korea, including the United States, Great Britain, Canada, France, Belgium, the Netherlands, Colombia, Ethiopia, South Africa, Australia, New Zealand, Turkey, Greece, Thailand, Philippines and Luxembourg. Four member nations, including Norway, Denmark, Sweden and India, sent medical units. Italy also sent its Red Cross, but it was not a member nation.

Seven non-member states sent aid, including the two occupied countries of Japan and Germany. While Japan was not a member state, its location made it a vital support base for the war, and it housed the closest remaining US personnel who could be transported to Korea. Germany notified the UN headquarters of its intent to set up a field hospital in South Korea in May 1953 to support UN soldiers participating in the Korean War; it sent a medical unit of around 80 staff the following year. It was not included among the Korean War providers of medical aid, however, because its medical support activities began after the armistice treaty was signed on 27 July 1953.

On 27 June 1950, the UN Security Council passed Resolution 83, obligating member nations to 'consider sending assistance to the Republic of Korea as may be necessary to repel the armed attack and to restore international peace and security in the area'. While US units (who committed the largest contingent and amount of aid to the war effort) had been in the country since President Truman ordered them in the wake of the North Korean invasion, UN ground forces began to trickle into Korea at the end of August 1950, starting with Commonwealth 27th Brigade, which aided in the defence of the Pusan Perimeter and the UN offensive to link in with the Inchon landings. The nations that followed represented the largest coalition in modern history to pledge to a common military and political endeavour. While that demonstration of humanity was commendable, it brought with it a unique set of problems.

The South Korean military was placed under US/UN control, whose troops came to be known as the Korean Augmentation to the United States Army, or KATUSA, soldiers. They were also later attached to British, Australian, Canadian, French and Belgian units. Interestingly enough, KATUSAs were augmented with US units before African-American and white

US soldiers served in integrated units. Moreover, non-US or Korean soldiers were sent as smaller battalion-size forces without a complete support structure. Because of this, they could not operate independently and were attached to US units. Britain, Canada and Turkey were the exception: each sent a brigade-sized force, comprising roughly 3000–5000 men.

Every UN and non-UN member nation had its own reason for participating in the Korean War. Despite the varied reasons,

Above: Men of the British No. 41 (Royal Marine) Commandos plant demolition charges along railroad tracks of an enemy supply line, 13km (eight miles) south of Songjin, 10 April 1951.

the real success was the vindication of the United Nations itself. And despite the differences that arose from the sheer number of different cultures involved, they had come together to fight for a common cause – a feat that had never been accomplished in relative scale or magnitude.

Above: September 1950: US Marines fight in the streets of Seoul against remaining North Korean forces controlling pockets of the city.

While MacArthur felt it prudent to issue news of success, the Marines spent the next two days mopping up enemy forces within Seoul. In these efforts, the city was badly scarred, and many parts were still burning days later.

On 29 September, MacArthur arrived at Kimpo Airfield from Tokyo and was escorted by Gen. Almond and other high-ranking generals to the National Assembly Hall in the Government House in Seoul. There, MacArthur entered with South Korean President Syngman Rhee and proclaimed in front of Korean officials, citizens and prominent military personnel:

> *Mr President: By the grace of a merciful Providence our forces fighting under the standard of the greatest hope and inspiration of mankind, the United Nations have liberated this ancient capital city of Korea…On behalf of the United*

Nations Command I am happy to restore you, Mr President, the seat of your government that from it you may better fulfill your constitutional responsibilities.

BREAKING THROUGH AT PUSAN

The Inchon operation had been vital not only to establishing a UN stronghold in Korea; it also had the effect of blunting the North Korean onslaught that had hitherto been too strong to stop. The entire operation from the landing at Inchon cost UN forces approximately 3500 casualties, with the heaviest of those from X Corps in the 1st Marine Division. The landing at Inchon had also succeeded in putting X Corps forces to the rear of North Korean forces. Doing so was vital not only to landing more supplies, but also in the greater plan to break out from the Pusan Perimeter.

Below: A US Air Force sergeant inspects rockets before they are loaded on a P-80 fighter jet at Itazuke Airbase, Japan. During the Korean War, Itazuke was a major combat airfield for the USAF.

The breakout and the Inchon landing were initially planned as operations that would begin simultaneously. Plans for the breakout changed, however, as Gen. Walker contemplated the realities of success. He planned instead to attack the day after the Inchon landing, taking advantage of a demoralized North Korean force. The Eighth US Army would attack northward to meet up with X Corps forces attacking southward.

After initially wavering on where to break from the Pusan Perimeter – the Eighth Army was severely undermanned, low on resources and wondered if a successful breakout could be made – two routes were decided on, both blocked by the North Korean Army. The main effort would utilize the highway from the Naktong River opposite Waegwan to Kumchon, and across the Sobaek Mountain Range to Taejon. If more routes were needed to complete the breakout, the valley of the Naktong River northwards to the Sang-ju area could be used.

In preparation for the breakout, the Far East Command reorganized the Eighth Army based on corps. Initially, the Eight

Below: ROK soldiers follow UN soldiers through the town of Inchon in the wake of the amphibious landings.

US Army had directly controlled four infantry divisions and other attached ground forces of regimental and brigade size. In the build-up for the breakout, the Eighth Army was provided two corps: I Corps and IX Corps. Walker grouped the main breakout forces under I Corps. Enemy forces along the entire perimeter stood at approximately 70,000.

The US Eighth Army strength stood at a little over 84,000, comprised of I Corps, the 1st Cavalry Division, the 24th Infantry Division, the US 2nd Division, the US 25th Division, the attached KATUSAs and the British 27th Infantry Brigade. ROK Army forces stood at just over 72,000, bringing the total UN contingent to more than 140,000 men. Such overwhelming numbers beg the question why UN forces were pinned down along the Pusan Perimeter.

> SUCH OVERWHELMING NUMBERS BEG THE QUESTION WHY UN FORCES WERE PINNED DOWN ALONG THE PUSAN PERIMETER.

While there were 140,000 men on the UN side, few of these were in the rifle companies that actually did the fighting. Some of these companies were down to 25 per cent of their authorized strength. The KATUSA forces that were attached to US units were raw, virtually untrained and not yet successfully integrated, which made them of little value in terms of combat. ROK armies also suffered heavy casualties among trained officer and non-commissioned officer ranks.

The operation began on 16 September. Success was elusive at first. Weather caused the planned Air Force B-29 saturation bombing to be called off, and in many sectors of the perimeter, the fighting resembled the attack/counter-attack situation that had characterized the fighting so far. In the first day, the only successes were the advancement of the 15th ROK Regiment of the 1st ROK Division along the right of the North Korean strongpoint north of Taegu and the 8-km (5-mile) breakout southward of the US 2nd Division to the hills looking over the Naktong River.

In the following days, the 2nd Division pushed enemy forces back across the river with the aid of heavy air attacks on enemy forces. The river crossing by the 38th Infantry (attached to the 2nd Infantry Division) was important: it marked the first

INTEGRATING FORCES

ALTHOUGH TURKEY SENT A brigade-sized force, its participation in the UN effort has become widely scrutinized. In October 1950, the 5000 men that made up the Turkish Brigade arrived in Korea. Turkey was not originally welcomed to the UN. Sitting on the border between Europe and the Middle East, it was not considered within the scope of what the European Recovery Act in the wake of World War II was established for.

In the Cold War, providing for a strong Western Europe to stave off the spread of communism was deemed to be of utmost importance. Turkey, however, was looking not necessarily to Westernize, but to loosen the control imposed by traditional Islamic governing practices, and looked to benefit from the redevelopment that was taking place after two world wars had ravaged Europe. By offering to send troops to Korea, it demonstrated a public commitment to wage war against communism and was accepted as a member of the United Nations. The Turkish presence among the UN forces, however, led to unique issues for the US units they were attached to.

Communication was the largest issue plaguing UN forces. British Commonwealth Forces were English-speaking, which created no issues for the US commanders who were leading the UN forces. Turkish, Greek, Norwegian, Thai, French, Spanish, Dutch, Swedish, Italian, and several regional languages, however, required translators, adding another layer of complexity in the planning and execution of the war. In the case of the Turkish Brigade, food and bathing also presented problems. As Muslims, they would not eat pork. They also preferred their own blend of strong coffee. Bathing, too, became difficult, as their modesty prevented them from showering in a communal setting.

To solve the problem, canned fish from Japan replaced pork and shower stalls were implemented so that more than one individual could shower at a time. These intricacies, while seemingly small, were a problem with many of the forces involved in the UN. The Thai forces only ate rice and boiled vegetables, while the Greeks did not eat corn or carrots and required olive oil for cooking. The Indians were mainly vegetarians, while the French, Belgians and Dutch usually ate more bread.

The list of differences was long. Even clothing posed a problem, as many of the Asian nations were smaller in stature than other participating nations – a situation that required careful attention. The US, as the lead nation in the coalition, had to devise a way to make the logistics work.

The greatest challenge, however, came from integrating ROK forces with the Eighth US Army. Prior to the breakout from the Pusan Perimeter and the Inchon landing, ROK units were kept together at the front and controlled by their own headquarters. When the Eighth Army was reorganized, ROK forces were attached to US forces. With the need for soldiers being acute, the KATUSA program was expanded drastically so that, by the time of the Inchon landing, more than 19,000 KATUSA soldiers were attached to the Eighth Army and X Corps.

Below: Ethiopian troops are instructed in a military intelligence class, May 1951. The Kagnew Infantry Battalion distinguished themselves on the battlefield during combat operations in the Old Baldy, Pork Chop Hill area.

Below: 10 September 1950: British and American troops greet each other on the Nakdong River as the Eighth US Army plans an offensive to break out from the Pusan Perimeter.

permanent river crossing by any unit of the Eighth Army in the breakout, and it occurred two days ahead of schedule.

The 2nd Division moves across the Naktong occurred simultaneously with attacks westward towards Waegwan by elements of the US 1st Cavalry. The 5th Regimental Combat Team moved through the hills east of the river, paving the way for remaining elements of the 1st Cavalry. In five days, it crushed the entire right flank and part of the centre of the North Korean 3rd Division, making it impossible for it to maintain its positions along the road to Taegu. The 24th Infantry Division was slated to cross the river first.

However, the crossing took time, as makeshift ferries and sturdier bridges had to be constructed first to cross the Kumho River, a tributary that stood between them and the Naktong. That hurdle, coupled with enemy mortar attacks from across the river, delayed plans for crossing. By 20 September, air strikes had suppressed enemy mortar and artillery positions across the river, and all three regiments of the 24th Infantry Division and the attached Commonwealth 27th Brigade were across the Naktong River. That was the extent of their early success in the breakout campaign.

> IN THE FOLLOWING DAYS, THE 2ND DIVISION PUSHED ENEMY FORCES BACK ACROSS THE RIVER WITH THE AID OF HEAVY AIR ATTACKS ON ENEMY FORCES.

BOGGED DOWN AT BATTLE MOUNTAIN

If the 2nd Division was the clear leader in the breakout campaign, the 25th Division on the north end of the UN line fared the worst. While the 2nd Division and 1st Cavalry were making progress, the 25th was unable to attack, and was still fighting enemy forces behind its lines. There, the North Koreans controlled the hills at Battle Mountain, Pil-bong and Sobuk-san, keeping the US 24th Infantry under constant attack and preventing other elements from moving forward. The 35th Division was tasked with assaulting Battle Mountain and Pilbong on 17–18 September.

Every time the hills were attacked, enemy automatic fire drove them back, with severe casualties. On the morning of 19 September, however, it was discovered that the North

Koreans had abandoned the crest at Battle Mountain. The US 24th Infantry moved up and occupied it while the 35th Infantry Regiment began to press forward and the 21st Infantry continued to fight to their left. As the 35th Infantry continued to press forward, they met abandoned enemy automatic firing positions scattered through the hills.

The sudden change in the push-and-pull fight that had consumed the northern position since the beginning of August made it clear that the enemy was retreating northward. The effects of the Inchon landing were apparent. The North Korean High Command had ordered the withdrawal of its main forces in the South and instructed them to move northward.

By 23 September, North Korean movement away from the Pusan Perimeter was in full swing. Gen. Walker followed the fleeing North Korean Army. His focus was clear: 'He planned to kill, capture, or drive off all of the North Korean Army from South Korea.' He understood that his Eighth Army would be beyond its logistical capabilities by the time it reached Seoul

Below: B-29s dropping ordnance over Korea. B-29s destroyed North Korea's strategic targets by 15 September 1950, prompting the NKPA to increase the number of anti-aircraft defences against them.

Above: An American tank crew watch South Koreans on the march near Taejon after the Eighth Army liberates the town on the drive towards Seoul.

and the border, so he focused on liberating Korea where he could until he was able to link up with the X Corps forces working southward.

The drive towards Seoul was made possible by the cover provided by the Fifth Air Force, which punished enemy forces, and the combined arms task forces formed by some of the ground divisions. Movement became more efficient and rapid due to truck-borne infantry following mobile artillery and tanks. By 29 September, much of the western half of South Korea had been taken by IX Corps. In the I corps area of operations, the 24th Division had broken up the North Korean defence around Kumchon and entered Taejon, capturing the straggling forces of the North Korean division that had been routed from the south.

The 2nd Infantry Division, after its breakout at Tabudong, headed north towards Seoul. In a week, I Corps had covered the same ground that had taken the North Korean Division almost two months to capture. The ROK army enjoyed great success in the last week of September as well. Finally winning the admiration of Gen. Walker, the ROK First Division mopped up enemy forces behind I Corps forces.

The breakout from Pusan and the subsequent push towards the 38th Parallel had been costly to both sides. Moreover, advancing Eighth Army forces came face to face with the horrors of the war as they passed the bodies of their men who were North Korean prisoners of war, executed in horrific ways. As UN units entered the towns of Mokpo, Hamyung, Chonju, Kongju and others along the route north, they also saw the bodies of hundreds of murdered men, women and children. Most of those civilians were families of ROK office holders, Christians, police officers, property owners, ROK soldiers and other counter-revolutionaries. Many were killed only because the North Koreans would not transport them on their retreat.

> SUSPECTING NORTH KOREAN INFILTRATORS MAY BE AMONG THE FLEEING SOUTH KOREAN PEASANTS, AMERICAN COMMANDERS HAD ORDERED UNITS ... TO SHOOT CIVILIANS AS A DEFENCE AGAINST DISGUISED ENEMY SOLDIERS.

During the retreat, the greatest atrocity occurred at Taejon, where, between 23 and 26 September, the North Korean police shot 5000 ROK soldiers, 40 American GIs and more than 5000 civilian hostages. As UN forces moved northwards, they could see the rotting corpses of those executed piled into trenches along the road.

The North Koreans were not the only ones to commit atrocities. One of the most significant atrocities committed by American soldiers was at No Gun Ri, a hamlet some 160km (100 miles) southeast of Seoul. Suspecting North Korean infiltrators may be among the fleeing South Korean peasants, American commanders had ordered units retreating through South Korea to shoot civilians as a defence against disguised enemy soldiers. The order from many commanders was that absolutely no refugees were to be taken and nobody was to breach American lines. At No Gun Ri, hundreds of Korean civilians were machine-gunned under a railroad bridge. Chun Choon Ja, 12 years old at the time, said: 'The American soldiers played with our lives like boys playing with flies.'

TAKING THE WAR NORTH

The decision to take the war into North Korea was not made in haste. As early as 21 September, President Truman had informed Gen. MacArthur that any such move would have to receive the approval of the United Nations. MacArthur wanted to press forward to unify Korea by force and let Syngman Rhee govern all of Korea. The Joint Chiefs of Staff back in Washington wanted a plan that called for the destruction of the Democratic People's Republic of Korea while that left Korea's future open.

On 26 September, MacArthur was informed that the United Nations Command could operate in North Korea so long as it was for the purpose of routing the enemy and not for an occupation. While UN forces marched north, Syngman Rhee would only have the power to govern south of the 38th Parallel. The other stipulation was that if Chinese or Russian forces intervened, then he should be prepared to receive and follow new directions, and that any move towards the Yalu River (the Chinese border) should be undertaken by ROK forces.

After re-establishing the government of South Korea on 29 September, MacArthur outlined a two-pronged offensive into North Korea to destroy enemy forces. He doubted that the Chinese or Russians would intervene and subsequently gave it no further thought in his planning. According to his plan, the Eighth Army would be responsible for the main effort – a drive on Pyongyang through Kaesong and Sariwon. X Corps,

Below: Trenches are filled with dead civilians massacred by retreating communist troops. Eighth Army forces were confronted by similar mass graves as they entered the towns of Mokpo, Hamyung, Chonju and Kongju along the route north.

which remained under his direct control, would board ships and land at Wonsan, where it would join ROK I Corps and anchor a United Nations advance to control the Pyongyang–Yondock–Wonsan line across Korea.

The eastern limit of the operation would move as far as Hungnam, but only ROK forces would operate north of that line. MacArthur had been working on the plan for two months and expected it to be complete between 15 and 20 October, depending on when Washington gave him the go-ahead.

The plan had some issues. The US Navy doubted it could clear Wonsan of the mines that blocked its harbour in two weeks or less. The Eighth Army did not possess the logistical support for such a rapid move north either. Gen. Walker had been the main opponent of the plan, partly because of his disdain for the X Corps commander Ned Almond, and partly because the logistics of such an endeavour seemed insurmountable under the current conditions. Walker and a few other commanders took these logistical concerns seriously, exercising caution. MacArthur, however, dismissed their concerns as trivial details that his forces would conquer – much like his dismissal of dissent in the planning for the Inchon landing.

On 1 October, MacArthur organized a public call for the North Korean armed forces to disband and abandon Kim Il-sung's failed regime. North Korean forces should prepare to surrender their arms and their prisoners of war to United Nations Command forces and then return to their homes to avoid more bloodshed. The message, coordinated with Washington, did not have the intended effect. Ten days later, Kim Il-sung made a radio speech calling for a defence of 'every inch of the Motherland'; a move that did not signal any desire to surrender.

In the south, Syngman Rhee began to fume over what he saw as a concerted effort to appease

Below: South Korean President Syngman Rhee (right) with US General Edward Craig. Craig commanded the highly effective 1st Marine Provisional Brigade during the Battle of the Pusan Perimeter.

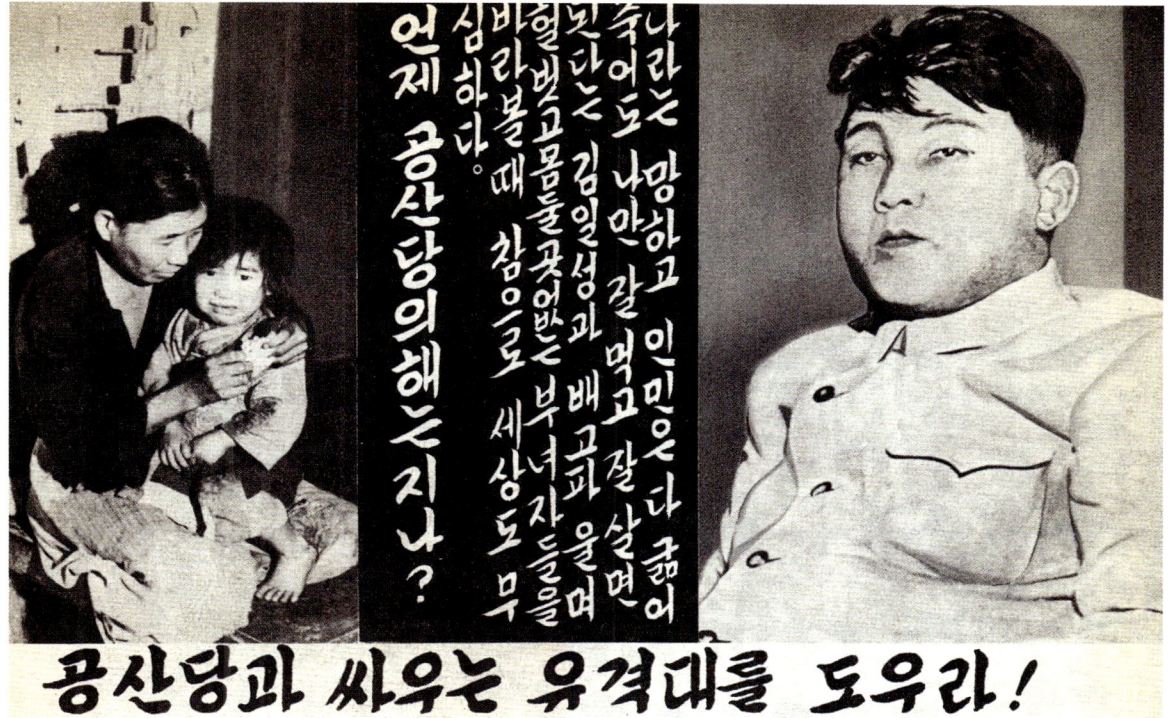

Above: A propaganda leaflet distributed by United Nations forces contrasting the communist leaders' luxury with the poverty of the average North Korean citizen. It shows a poorly-clothed and starving mother and child juxtaposed with the well-fed leader of North Korea, Kim Il-sung.

China. He understood that his government was not popular with the United Nations Command on Korea and many of the most influential UN members. Rhee, however, ordered ROK soldiers across the 38th Parallel. As they encountered executed South Korean hostages and learned of more missing people, Rhee's heart filled with bloodlust. He planned to send governors and police into northern Korea to take control and conduct a political cleansing. He wanted North Korea integrated with the Republic of Korea with bullets and ballots, and without the supervision of any United Nations agency. Given his outspoken point of view towards their authority, it was no surprise that members of the UN did not believe that the Rhee government should dictate the terms of unification.

If Rhee left doubts in the mind of the UN, so too did President Truman's lack of control of Gen. MacArthur. Wary leaders of the United Nations, including Great Britain and India, doubted that MacArthur would follow any guidance from Washington, given that Truman had failed to summon the courage to issue him direct orders hitherto. Their main concern still centred on avoiding a war with China as a result of the pursuit of the NKPA forces towards its border. After much political jockeying between MacArthur, Washington, Rhee and the UN, MacArthur ordered the Eighth Army to carry out the occupation mission. Interestingly enough, his order preceded actual approval.

EIGHTH ARMY SUCCESS

October ushered in a period of resounding victory for the United Nations Command. The two divisions of ROK I Corps marched and fought remaining elements of the KPA 5th Division and entered Wonsan on 11 October. The Fifth Air Force resupplied ROK 3rd Division as it awaited the arrival of X Corps. The Capital Division followed the mountain roads and amassed outside Wonsan to join in attacks to clean up the city. ROK II Corps crossed the border on 6–7 October and occupied the critical connection of valleys, corridors and roads known as the 'Iron Triangle'.

The major advance came from the US I Corps, with three regiments of the 1st Cavalry Division abreast, the ROK First Division on the right, and the 24th Infantry Division and the Commonwealth 27th Brigade bringing up the rear echelon, ready to slide left. By 13–14 October, I Corps had broken through North Korean border defences, and the 1st Cavalry Division and ROK 1st Division headed for Pyongyang.

If the Eighth Army's move northwards was a success, the X Corps amphibious landing at Wonsan proved to be ill planned. First, the 1st Marine Division assault required a week to organize, meaning that it only left Inchon on the day it was supposed to arrive in Wonsan. Inchon Harbour itself proved to be the main issue. Its limited port could not handle the combined traffic of taking out X Corps and serving as the point of entry for supplies being routed to the Eighth Army. The 7th Infantry Division, also supposed to use Inchon, moved its forces south to Pusan by motor against the flow of traffic headed north. It fought

> IF THE EIGHTH ARMY'S MOVE NORTHWARDS WAS A SUCCESS, THE X CORPS AMPHIBIOUS LANDING AT WONSAN PROVED TO BE ILL PLANNED.

Opposite: USAF B-26 Invader aircraft attack warehouses and docks at Wonsan. Petroleum refineries, shipbuilding, railways and chemical facilities were the first targets as UN forces attempted to pound North Korea into submission.

Above: A small Korean child sits alone in the street, after elements of the 1st Marine Division and South Korean marines invaded the city of Inchon, September 1950.

its way through two major ambushes, only to reach Pusan and ships that were ill equipped to land at Wonsan.

Despite numerous issues in the south in trying to get to Wonsan, Wonsan itself presented major problems. The port offered excellent capabilities, but reaching it was problematic. As indicated earlier, the North Koreans and Russians had blocked Wonsan's restricted channels with an estimated 3000 moored and floating mines. US Navy Admirals Joy, Strubbe, Doyle and Burke had told Gen. Wright and Gen. Almond (in charge of planning) that X Corps could reach Wonsan sooner by marching overland behind the ROK I Corps. Instead of taking those suggestions to MacArthur, Almond and Wright proposed that that Task Force 90 (the Wonsan operation) should go farther north to Hungnam. Hungnam, however, was also mined. After two weeks of using

US, Korean and Japanese minesweepers, underwater demolition experts, naval aviation, and even local fishermen, a narrow passage through the channel was accomplished on 25 October.

WAKE ISLAND

While the Wonsan operation was underway and the navy was working desperately to clear a passage, President Truman and Gen. MacArthur flew out to an arranged meeting at Wake Island on 15 October. Truman had made an earlier request to see MacArthur in Washington or Honolulu, but MacArthur thought that too far from his principal area of concern.

The meeting served two goals: (1) To assess the policies that would flow from the approaching victory and (2), to provide a media event that allowed them to share that victory. The idea was devised by Washington officials; they wanted Truman to be presented more as a commander-in-chief figure than someone who fell second behind the reputation of MacArthur. A full day of group talks and a private president–MacArthur session would address current operations, rehabilitation in Korea, and future relations with Japan, Formosa, Indochina and China.

MacArthur wasted no time in taking the stage. After assuring Truman that he would advance the plans set forth by Washington and not other political motivations, he launched into a two-hour tirade about occupation, nation-building and internal security. All signs pointed to the belief that the war was already won. Truman asked MacArthur about Chinese or Russian intervention, to which he responded, that 'no, they had missed their chance. IF the Chinese in Manchuria marched, there would be the greatest slaughter administered by Far East Air Forces. Soviet air could not stop an air offensive on the Chinese army.'

MacArthur reassured Truman 'that victory was won in Korea, that Japan was ready for a peace treaty, and that the Chinese communists would not attack.' After the meeting was concluded, Truman read a press release before boarding a

> THE NORTH KOREANS AND RUSSIANS HAD BLOCKED WONSAN'S RESTRICTED CHANNELS WITH AN ESTIMATED 3000 MOORED AND FLOATING MINES.

plane home that expressed his satisfaction with the conference, MacArthur and the progress of the war. He stressed Korea's need for reconstruction. The trip had accomplished what it intended. Truman's goal for peace in Asia and the simultaneous demonstration of his control over MacArthur impressed US and foreign media and leaders.

GEN. ALMOND ALSO EXPECTED TO ADD THE 3RD INFANTRY DIVISION TO X CORPS, BRINGING ITS COMBINED STRENGTH TO 85,000 TROOPS.

TOWARDS THE YALU

By 28 October, the 1st Marine Division had landed at Wonsan. They marched north to Hungnam, where the minesweeping operations had moved to clear the harbour. There they met with 7th Infantry Division, who had finally made it to the north. Gen. Almond also expected to add the 3rd Infantry Division to X Corps, bringing its combined strength to 85,000 troops. On 26 October, Almond began to shift his forces around so that the 1st Marine Division and 7th Infantry Divisions could move northwest into the interior to find remaining North Korean resistors.

During the same period, a final drive by I Corps on Pyongyang commenced. After the collapse of fighting in the Kumchon pocket on 15 October, the 5th Cavalry and the Commonwealth 27th Brigade took the lead for the 1st Cavalry and the 24th Infantry Divisions. The main advance units of the 5th Cavalry and the ROK 1st Division reached the Taedong River and the main bridge into Pyongyang on 19 October. The next day, Gen. Paik led ROK forces across the river, reached the Democratic Republic of Vietnam's capitol building, and blocked the major highway to the north. For the

Below: US President Harry Truman and General Douglas MacArthur meet on Wake Island after the success of the Inchon landings and recapture of Seoul to discuss achieving a 'political victory' in Korea.

COMMONWEALTH 27TH BRIGADE

Above: Men of the 3rd Battalion, Royal Australian Regiment (3 RAR), hitch a ride on board a Centurion tank while crossing a pontoon bridge spanning the Imjin River, June 1951.

FORMED IN 1948 AND sent to Korea in 1950, the Commonwealth 27th Brigade first went into action during the defence of the Pusan Perimeter on 29 August 1950, and the UN offensive to link with the Inchon landings. The brigade was joined in September 1950 by an Australian contingent, 3rd Battalion, Royal Australian Regiment (3 RAR), and in December 1950 by the 2nd Battalion, Princess Patricia's Canadian Light Infantry. It would continue to play a vital role in the UN mission in Korea and fight in the retreat from the Yalu River, the Chinese Winter and the UN counter-offensive. The brigade was joined by the specially raised 16 Field Regiment Royal New Zealand Artillery in January 1951, and then a Canadian infantry battalion in February. The brigade's final action was during the Battle of Kapyong in April 1951. Both the Argylls and Middlesex Regiment were relieved and the brigade was disbanded, to be replaced by the fully constituted 28th British Commonwealth Infantry Brigade, part of the 1st Commonwealth Division.

Below: This Republic of Korea (ROK) soldier shows his indebtedness to US supplies. His clothing is the US M1943 battledress, a uniform that worked on a layering system. The outer layers had good properties of wind- and rain-resistance, while inner layers provided warmth. The US M1 helmet is worn on top of a woollen cap. He is armed with an M1 carbine.

Opposite: Soldiers of the US 1st Cavalry Division make their way across a railway bridge spanning the Taedong River near Pyongyang.

next week, Syngman Rhee attempted to establish control over the whole of Korea, while the UN remained steadfast in its position that the Rhee government should not be allowed to govern north of the 38th Parallel.

The Eighth Army had to establish a civil assistance program to address unification issues and preserve order. US leaders realized that any real attempt to establish order would have to incorporate some contingent of ROK administrators, but not enough to draw reappraisal from the UN. On 28 October, President Rhee and a small official party visited Pyongyang. Pledging his support to the UN plan for relief and recovery in front of liberated Koreans, he urged peace, patience and obedience to the US Army authorities. He knew that the US Army needed South Korean assistance in policing despite UN desires, and saw it not as a temporary situation but as a stepping stone to outright control of Korea.

With Pyongyang secure, MacArthur looked to move north towards the Yalu River, the demarcation between North Korea and China. He visited Pyongyang on 21 October to confer with Gen. Walker and Gen. Stratemeyer on how to handle coordination issues. Original plans assumed that the only outstanding challenge was to mop up remaining enemy forces. Intelligence reports had identified Sinuiju as the North Koreans' main rallying point. Fifth Air Force aircraft had also reported seeing hundreds of vehicles heading towards Sinuiju on the last day of the campaign for Pyongyang. Gen. Walker, senior Navy Admirals and Fifth Air Force Gen. Partridge urged caution on the drive north. MacArthur, as always, was not persuaded.

MacArthur received accurate intelligence reports that the North Koreans had evacuated GI prisoners and many Korean soldiers and civilians to the north as hostages. On 19 October, he ordered the 187th Regimental Combat Team to assault the

west coast road junctions of Sukchon and Sunchon, 48km (30 miles) north of Pyongyang. It was the first operation north of Pyongyang. While the 187th found no POWs, they did meet more enemy fighters than they could handle alone. This served as the catalyst to the northward movement of the Eighth Army and X Corps towards to the Chinese border.

MacArthur, urged on by forward momentum and the vindication of his decision to move northwards, decided to change the policy of placing South Korean troops in the forefront of the advance to the Yalu – a decision that drew a reminder from the Joint Chiefs of Staff of their earlier directive that only ROK troops should appear along the border.

MacArthur, as energetic as ever to fight back against the JCS, used his letter issued the previous month from Secretary of Defense George C. Marshall stating that he should feel unhampered in his operations to destroy the North Korean forces. He also cited Truman's praise for him at Wake Island as his latest authorization for operations in North Korea. He did inform the JCS that he understood their concerns, however, and would continue to watch for Chinese or Russian intervention.

Gen. Walker and Gen. Almond, the two principal commanders in North Korea, responded to MacArthur's order to advance in different ways. Gen. Walker ordered the Commonwealth 27th Brigade up the Sinanju coast road towards the Yalu estuary. The ROK 1st Division advanced north towards Unsan, while the 187th Regimental Combat Team and 1st Calvary Division remained between the river and Pyongyang. Walker exercised little control over ROK II Corps, whose elements spread east to west and attacked north towards the river, with the

> GEN. WALKER AND GEN. ALMOND, THE TWO PRINCIPAL COMMANDERS IN NORTH KOREA, RESPONDED TO MACARTHUR'S ORDER TO ADVANCE IN DIFFERENT WAYS.

Below: The 38th Parallel demarcation set up by the 728th Military Police Battalion, who were in combat during the war and later assisted in traffic control and various other law enforcement duties.

ROK 7th Infantry scoring a victory at Chonan. ROK forces left a company to patrol the river, but most retreated to Chosan to begin their celebration.

Almond, unlike Walker, fully intended to acquiesce to MacArthur's order to let US forces take the lead. His challenge, then, was replacing the ROK I Corps with his own 1st Marine Division and 7th Infantry Division along the east coast. The ROK 3rd Division would hold at Wonsan and push west towards the Eighth Army boundary along the Taebaek Mountains, while the 1st Marine Division would replace the Capital Division in the Hamhung–Hungnam area. The ROK division would occupy Iwon and hold it for the 7th Infantry Division's arrival. By 25 October, one regiment of the ROK 3rd Division advanced 48km (30 miles) inland to the hydroelectric plant at the base of the Changjin (Chosin) Reservoir, where they captured a soldier who claimed to be a Chinese regular. Since the 7th Marines were on their way to the same area, X Corps headquarters found no cause for concern.

So it was that, by the end of October 1950, the United Nations Command stood on the brink of a complete victory against North Korean forces. Or did they? While MacArthur and his always eager-to-follow X Corps commander Gen. Almond felt complete confidence in the control of their position, none of the other principal ground commanders echoed the same sentiments. Only time would tell if UN forces had indeed won the war, or if they were merely staring down the face of an enemy onslaught.

Above: British machine gunners cover the advance of infantry at Chongju as part of the advance towards the Yalu River, 29 October 1950.

CHINESE INTERVENTION

3

The fall of Pyongyang, the North Korean capital, had been a significant development in the war. Previous orders to the NKPA forces to invade the Republic of Korea and subsequent military decisions were all generated in Pyongyang. Its demise meant that the North Koreans were on the defensive and, to the UN forces, signalled that victory was nearly at hand.

UN FORCES continued to push north towards the Yalu River and the Chinese border in an offensive that spread east to west throughout the country, spurred on by Gen. MacArthur's removal of restrictions on their advance. While the US president and his government officials wished to avoid bringing the Chinese into the war, each victory against the NKPA provided MacArthur with further vindication in his struggle with Washington and a Joint Chiefs of Staff (JCS) who he felt did not understand the true situation in Korea. To his consternation, in the last week of October 1950, the Chinese crossed the Yalu River, blunting the UN offensive simultaneously across its front, and completely surprising UN forces and MacArthur himself.

Opposite: A war-weary Korean girl trudges by a stalled M-26 tank with her brother on her back at Haengju, north of Seoul by the Han River, 9 June 1951.

Above: Captain Emil Kapaun (right), with Headquarters Company, 8th Cavalry Regiment, helps carry an exhausted soldier away from the battlefield. Kapaun, a Catholic chaplain, died in a prisoner-of-war camp in 1951.

UNSAN

Unsan was in the eastern section of North P'yongan province, roughly 60km (37 miles) northeast of the North Korean capital of Pyongyang. Between 25 October and 4 November 1950, Unsan was the site of one of the most devastating battles for US forces in the Korean War. On 25 October, the ROK 1st Infantry Division attacked what they thought were remnants of the KPA at Unsan. Soon after, captured Chinese soldiers alerted the ROK soldiers to a 10,000-strong Chinese force waiting north of Unsan to join the fight. ROK forces fought for positions in the surrounding hills around Unsan, but by the following morning they found themselves surrounded by enemy forces from the north and to the west, on the road between Unsan and Yongsan-dong.

The US 6th Medium Tank Battalion and the US 10th Anti-Aircraft Artillery Group were ordered to provide air support to ROK troops trying to break through Chinese lines to little avail. Gen. Walton Walker of the Eighth United States Army ordered the US 8th Cavalry Regiment of the US 1st Cavalry Division to fight with the ROK 15th Regiment in a northern attack.

The US 8th Cavalry Regiment had taken up positions around the town, its 1st Battalion defending the north of Unsan by the Samtan River, while its 2nd and 3rd Battalions defended the areas west of Unsan by the Nammyon River. Lack of UN manpower, however, created a 1.6-km (1-mile) gap between the 1st and 2nd Battalions, which Chinese forces exploited on 1 November. By later that night, the ROK 15th

> ROK FORCES FOUGHT FOR POSITIONS IN THE SURROUNDING HILLS AROUND UNSAN, BUT BY THE FOLLOWING MORNING THEY FOUND THEMSELVES SURROUNDED.

Infantry Regiment had been decimated and the US 1st and 2nd Battalions were low on ammunition. UN forces were ordered to withdraw by Maj. Gen. Frank W. Milburn, commander of the US I Corps.

The UN withdrawal from Unsan proved difficult, as Chinese forces continued to pour into the gap between the 1st and 2nd Battalions of the US 8th Calvary Regiment. Surrounded by the 347th and 348th Regiments of the PVA 116th Division, US forces had to mount an escape by infiltrating the Chinese lines and abandoning most of their vehicles and heavy weapons along the way. They managed to reach UN lines the following day.

Their brethren in the 3rd Battalion of the US 8th Cavalry were not so fortunate. Left alone during the night while Chinese forces were attacking the 1st and 2nd Battalions, a company of Chinese commandos from the 116th Division disguised as ROK soldiers infiltrated the 3rd Battalion command post and caught them in a surprise attack that killed many while they slept. After being pinned down, US 5th Cavalry Regiment was ordered to mount rescue attempts. The US 5th Calvary Regiment lost 350 soldiers in attacks against the PVA 343rd Regiment in their efforts to help, but were eventually ordered to retreat. Soldiers of the 3rd Battalion (8th Cavalry) continued to endure attacks from Chinese forces until fewer than 200 made it to UN lines on 4 November.

AUSTRALIAN ADVANCEMENTS

While the Chinese were finding success against the US and ROK forces at Unsan, the 27th British Commonwealth Brigade was fighting in a simultaneous effort against the Chinese invasion in the Central Mountains between 27 and 31 October. The leading

Below: November 1950: A Sherman tank laden with Australian soldiers 80km (50 miles) north of Pyongyang heads towards the Central Mountains and the Yalu River.

battalion of the composite forces that made up the 27th was 3 Battalion Royal Australian Regiment (3 RAR). As UN forces continued their drive towards the Yalu River in the preceding week, the 3 RAR had fought a significant battle at Yongju, otherwise known as the Battle of the Apple Orchard.

Racing north to link up with American paratroopers who had dropped ahead of the advance, the battalion was suddenly fired upon by an element of 239th Regiment of the KPA hidden in an apple orchard beside the road. C Company fixed bayonets and, with US Sherman tanks in support, swept through the enemy position. After a three-hour fight, the KPA began to retreat.

On 25 October, 3 RAR came up against the Taeryong River. A patrol crossed the partly demolished bridge and discovered the enemy in strength on the far side. In the search for an alternative crossing point, D Company captured the town of Pakchon further north along the river. That night, A and B Companies crossed the 'broken bridge' and dug in on the far side. They were soon detected by the KPA, who were determined not to allow the Australians to establish a bridgehead.

Several attacks were made on A and B Companies, who were reinforced by a platoon from C Company. At one point, a T-34 tank approached in the dark to within 10m (33ft) of the B Company Headquarters. American tanks were unable to cross the river to help the Australians. Nevertheless, the position was held, and at dawn the KPA called off their attack and withdrew.

Two days later, on 27 October, Chinese forces attacked in the Central Mountain region at Chonju. While 3 RAR were leading the Commonwealth 27th Brigade patrol through the area on 28 October, a battalion-sized KPA force, with tank and artillery support, was found dug in on wooded hills across the line of advance. US airstrikes softened the position before the 3RAR attacked. D Company took the ridge south of the road first and then A Company took the heights north of the road. Opposition was unexpectedly strong, but by dark, the Australians were dug in on

Below: An Australian soldier tries to keep warm by staying bundled up. The Aussie slouch hat he is wearing was designed for warmer climates, not the bitterly cold conditions that were characteristic of Korea in late 1950.

ROYAL AUSTRALIAN REGIMENT

THIS SOLDIER IS A member of the 3rd Battalion, Royal Australian Regiment. He wears the wide-brimmed slouch hat characteristic of Australian ground troops. British and US influences run through the rest of his outfit and equipment. The jacket and trousers are from the US M1943 combat dress; they are made of a light windproof and rain-resistant material, with warmth coming from the standard Australian fatigues worn underneath, the leather gloves and the thick wool scarf. The brown leather boots are worn with a pair of US-style gaiters secured by two buckle straps on each gaiter. British Commonwealth associations come through in the webbing (British 1937-pattern) and the weapons.

their objectives. The KPA counter-attacked to recover the ridges. D and A Companies were attacked by tanks and knocked out three of them with bazookas. The situation was so desperate that supporting artillery and mortar fire was called in within metres of the Australian fighting pits to break the attack. The fighting at Chongju was so intense that it has been recorded as the hardest fight that any Commonwealth troops had seen since they entered the war.

ASSAULT AND COUNTER-ATTACK

Hitherto, the Australians had only fought against the North Korean forces and had fared well. Having successfully captured Chongju on 30 October 1950, the Australians and their British counterparts were ordered to move back to Pakchon to provide reinforcement to the western flank of the United States Eighth Army. Following their success at Unsan against the Americans, the Chinese 117th Division of the 39th Army had attacked southward, intending to cut off the UN forces as they withdrew. They were tasked with defending the banks of Chongchon and Taeryong rivers.

On 4 and 5 November 1950, the communist forces launched a massive assault against the US 24th Infantry Division, pushing them back by about 2km (1.25 miles). The communist forces then turned west and advanced into the area between the Chongchon and Taeryong rivers in an effort to threaten the positions taken by the Commonwealth 27th Brigade.

The British and Australians successfully counter-attacked the Chinese forces occupying a number of nearby ridgelines during the day, but were in turn counter-attacked before being pushed off the high ground during the night. In their first battle with the Chinese, the 3 RAR captured a well-defended hill with only limited offensive support, and held it in the face of heavy counter-attacks before confused command decisions resulted in a disorganized night withdrawal while still in contact.

The withdrawal threatened to open the 27th British Commonwealth Brigade's left flank, and the Australians were ordered to immediately reposition on the ridge, yet ultimately it was too late to regain the feature in darkness. However, following heavy fighting, the pressure on the Australians unexpectedly ceased after midnight, and parties of Chinese were observed beginning to withdraw. By early morning, the Chinese attack had been checked and 3 RAR had redeployed to new positions in the paddy fields around the railway crossing north of Maenjung-dong.

Below: Men of the Argyll and Sutherland Highlanders take cover as they advance into the town of Chonju. As members of the 27th Commonwealth Brigade, the Highlanders were instrumental in the fighting between the Chongchon and Taeryong rivers.

TURKISH BRIGADE

Above: A Turkish soldier dug-in for the Battle of Kunu-ri in late November 1950. Fighting in the snow, the Turkish Brigade was attached to the US 25th Infantry Division.

ATTACHED TO THE US 25th Infantry Division, the Turkish Brigade fought in several actions. One of the major engagements in which it was involved was the battle of Kunu-ri. On 27 November 1950, east of Wawon, the leading Turkish party was ambushed by the Chinese and suffered a major defeat. Survivors of the leading Turkish party appeared in the zone of the American 38th Infantry north and northwest of the Wawon road the next day.

The Turks lost most of their equipment, vehicles and artillery, and sustained casualties of up to 1000 dead or wounded after fighting with the Chinese forces with superior numbers around the Kaechon and Kunu-ri area and the Tokchon-Kunu-ri road. Although the Turkish Brigade was cut off when they were encircled by Chinese regiments, they were still able to breach the Chinese trap and rejoin the US 2nd Infantry Division. The delay of the Chinese advance after meeting with heavy Turkish resistance helped UN forces to withdraw without suffering many casualties and reassemble later in December.

THE TURKS AT THE BATTLE OF WAWON

Beginning on 21 November, the 1st Turkish Brigade went into combat in its first real engagement since World War I. Two days prior, on 19 November, the US 25th Division left Kaesong and bedded down at Kunu-ri. The next day, the Turkish Brigade, which was largely an infantry unit without trucks for troop transport, was detached and reassigned to the IX Corps reserve at Kunu-ri. IX Corps consisted of the US 2nd and 25th Divisions and the 1st Turkish Brigade; the ROK 6th, 7th and 8th divisions; and the 1st Cavalry Division in Army reserve.

The Chinese had moved large contingents into the area. Standing in front of IX Corps to the west was the 180,000-man XIII Army Group of the Chinese Fourth Field Army. If that number was not ominous on its own, the 120,000-man IX Army Group of the Chinese Third Field Army stood against the US I Corps in the east. Total Chinese strength was about 300,000 men, and 12 divisions of the NKPA added approximately 65,000 men to the enemy strength.

Eighth Army forces were effectively split down the middle by the Chongchon River. As IX Corps moved northward, the Turks were ordered on 21 November to move north with the 25th Division. By 22 November 1950, the Turks had completed their assignment of neutralizing North Korean patrols in their allocated area. Advancing along with their American counterparts, the Turks were ordered to establish contact with the US 2nd Division on the right flank of the IX Corps and also to cover the right flank and rear of their division. The brigade had received information concerning a Chinese regiment known to be northwest of Tokchon.

On 26 November, the Chinese Communist Forces (CCF) launched strong counter-attacks against the US I Corps and IX Corps. The main Chinese force moved down the central mountain ranges against the ROK II Corps at Tokchon. The South Koreans could not withstand the attack and their defences collapsed. The Turks were ordered to protect the UN

BY 22 NOVEMBER 1950, THE TURKS HAD COMPLETED THEIR ASSIGNMENT OF NEUTRALIZING NORTH KOREAN PATROLS IN THEIR AREA.

Opposite: Turkish soldiers search Chinese prisoners after an engagement in December 1950 after the Battle of Wawon.

right flank. Trucks were assigned to transport the Turks' 1st Battalion to Wawon, 24km (15 miles) east of Kunu-ri, about halfway to Tokchon, unload and return for the 2nd Battalion. After insufficient trucks arrived, some of the brigade set out on foot. Orders, counter-orders and unclear transmissions made the situation worse. The Turks were ordered to close the road and secure Unsong-ni. The Turks soon found themselves in an undesirable position. General Yazici, commander of the Turkish forces, claimed that:

There was no time to move the brigade to Unsong-ni and deploy it there before dark... the enemy, which was supposed to be at Chongsong-ni, was in fact too close to the line which the Corps wanted us to hold. That the Brigade might be subjected to a surprise attack before reaching its position

Below: Turks march prisoners back to their command post after the battle of Kunu-ri as more troops move up to engage the enemy.

was highly probable. Even more important was the fact that the civilian population had not been moved out of the area. If the peasants and the guerrillas that might have been infiltrated among them attempted to block the mountain crossing or the Wawon Pass in the rear, the Brigade might suffer heavily. As a matter of fact, the 2nd Division, of which we were supposed to defend the right flank, was withdrawing. It was impossible to fulfil the task from Karil L'yong, where the Brigade was, because the terrain was very rugged and thickly wooded. In order to protect the Kunu-ri Tokchon road and the other roads to the north and the south, a 12-mile-wide front had to be held. This was impossible against a numerically superior enemy who knew the region well. Further, the terrain restricted the effective use of artillery and heavy infantry weapons.

Having to withdraw to the southeast, the Turks found their position on their east flank too exposed. Gen. Yazici ordered his men to move and position themselves at Wawon. During the move towards Wawon, the Turks lost communications with the US 2nd Division. When communications were reestablished, the Turks received intelligence that air observers had seen hundreds of Chinese moving towards Tokchon.

When they reached Wawon, they attacked towards Tokchon, on foot and without tank support. The terrain was upstream along the Tongjukkyo River into the mountain divide that separated the Chongchon River from the Taedong drainage. Two platoons of the Turkish Brigade assigned reconnaissance duty were now given rear-guard duty. The Chinese followed the brigade closely. The reconnaissance unit engaged the oncoming Chinese at the Karil L'yong Pass but was unable to break contact.

SUCCESSFUL DEFENCE

Although many Turks had fallen in this first engagement, they had successfully tied down the enemy. The Chinese suffered heavy casualties trying repeatedly to take the Turkish position, and all their attacks were repelled. Finally, Yazici, understanding that the brigade was being encircled by the numerically superior Chinese, ordered withdrawal.

The engulfing enemy constantly changed tactics and directions. Communications resumed with the Turkish Brigade, but there was difficulty in understanding the order received. The brigade was ordered to merge with the US 38th Regiment, cover the 38th's flank and secure a retreat route westward. In the confusion of the retreat and the garbled, misdirected and delayed messages, that crucial directive was two hours late in delivery. The column got turned about in the mass confusion and congestion of the road.

As the Turks approached Wawon, they encountered heavy enemy fire. The CCF had arrived before the Turks were able to reassemble and assume defensive positions. The Chinese

> WHEN COMMUNICATIONS WERE REESTABLISHED, THE TURKS RECEIVED INTELLIGENCE THAT AIR OBSERVERS HAD SEEN HUNDREDS OF CHINESE MOVING TOWARDS TOKCHON.

Above: November 1950: Master Sergeant George Miller selects human blood for a patient at the 8076th Mobile Army Surgical Hospital (M.A.S.H.) at Kunu-ri, Korea.

assaulted the ragged column and the soldiers were ordered to turn about once again. The Turkish 9th Company took the brunt of the attack as it covered for the retreating main body. The 10th Company of the brigade's 3rd Battalion received orders to form the brigade's general outpost line. Maj. Lutfu Bilgin, commander of the 3rd Battalion, sent his 9th Company to defend the 10th and 11th companies' flank.

The Chinese eased off on the 10th but continued to pound the 9th and 11th. On 28 November, roughly midway through the morning, the Chinese broke through and attacked the 9th's position in force. The company was overrun, and Major Bilgin and many of his men were killed.

Enemy reinforcements tried to encircle the entire brigade. Gen. Yazici, however, assessed the situation and took steps to protect his flank and avoid encirclement. The CCF poured forward, and the Turks were caught in the trap that the Chinese were laying. Suddenly, the Chinese broke off after encountering strong resistance of the 3rd Battalion.

During the withdrawal, the Chinese had attacked the Turks with overwhelming force and the brigade took such high casualties that by 30 November it was destroyed as a battleworthy unit. The only support the Turks received from IX Corps was a tank platoon and truck transportation. That was added to the brigade's artillery and enabled some of the brigade to survive.

At the 2nd Division Headquarters, information about the Turks and their actual movements was more and more difficult to obtain. Communication issues seemed to plague UN efforts in both directions. The tanks sent towards the Turks' position were repeatedly turned back. Confusion led to startling events, such as American soldiers simply abandoning their positions and equipment, including their weapons. The Chinese appeared to be everywhere and nowhere at the same time. Confirmation of Chinese movements was sparse and often erroneous. The Chinese, reported to be just ahead, turned out to be advancing on the soldiers from behind. The Turks decided to evacuate the command post.

Below: US Marines in winter gear as they fight entrenched Chinese troops during the Battle of Chosin Reservoir. More than 150,000 soldiers of the Chinese Ninth Army Group attacked Marine Corps units attached to X Corps.

BATTLE ON THE CHONGCHON RIVER AND THE CHANGJIN (CHOSIN) RESERVOIR

If the initial wave of the Chinese assault caught UN forces off-guard, the second phase of their offensive towards the end of November further demonstrated their position of importance in the war and drove the UN line further south. Despite the first phase campaign, UN leaders maintained that the Chinese had not responded in large force. In response to the successful Chinese First Phase Campaign against UN forces, Gen. MacArthur launched the Home-by-Christmas Offensive to expel the Chinese forces from Korea and end the war.

With a reconstituted ROK II Corps placed on the Eighth Army's right flank, the advance was led by US I Corps to the west, US IX Corps in the centre and ROK II Corps to the east. The three UN Corps advanced cautiously in a continuous front line in order to prevent more ambushes similar to the Chinese First Phase Campaign, but the lack of manpower stretched the UN forces to the limit.

> THE CHINESE APPEARED TO BE EVERYWHERE AND NOWHERE AT THE SAME TIME. CONFIRMATION OF CHINESE MOVEMENTS WAS SPARSE AND OFTEN ERRONEOUS.

Except for the strong PVA resistance against ROK II Corps, the Eighth Army met little opposition, and the line between Chongju to Yongwon was occupied on the night of 25 November. As the Eighth Army stopped its advance on the afternoon of 25 November 1950, the PVA 13th Army commenced their second phase attack in a massive frontal assault against the entire UN line from Yongsan-dong to Yongdong-ni. To the west, the ROK 1st Infantry Division of US I Corps was attacked by the PVA 66th Corps at Yongsan-dong. In the centre, strong probing actions by the PVA 39th and 40th Corps were carried out against US IX Corps at Ipsok and Kujang-dong. In the east, the PVA 38th and 42nd Corps broke through ROK II Corps' line at Tokchon and Yongdong-ni. The Home-by-Christmas Offensive stalled completely on the morning of 26 November.

Fighting continued at Kujang-dong, Ipsok, Yongsan-dong and Kunu-ri. On 28 November, Gen. MacArthur started to realize,

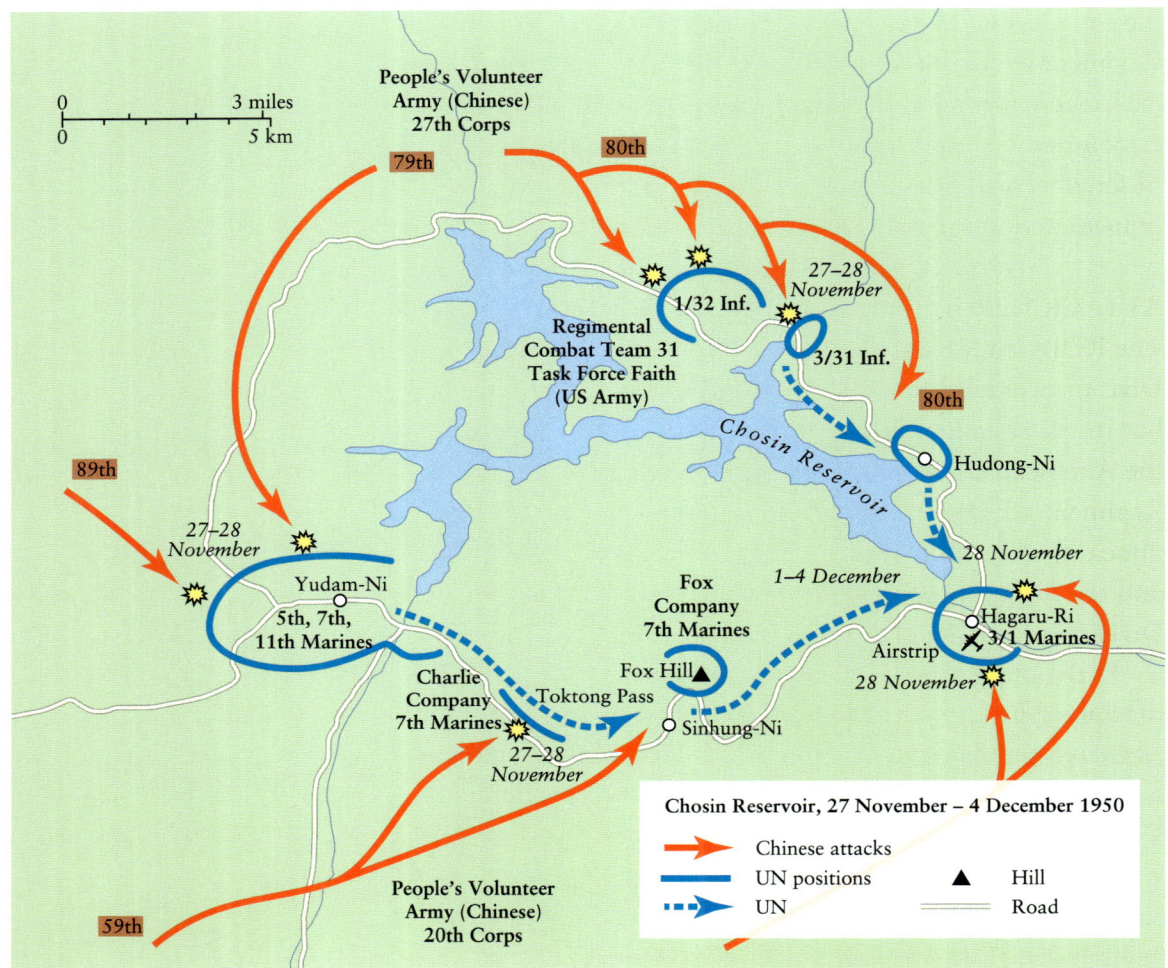

Above: At Chosin Reservoir, a UN force of 30,000 was encircled by 120,000 PVA troops. The Chinese 20th and 27th Corps launched multiple attacks on the night of 27 November along the road between the reservoir and Yudam-ni.

despite his earlier musings that UN forces would not run into serious trouble, that the war in Korea was not going well. With the start of the Battle of Chosin Reservoir on 27 November, MacArthur gathered his field commanders, including Walker, for a conference in Tokyo. During the conference, MacArthur learned about the situation on the Eighth Army's right flank and judged that the Eighth Army was in great danger. He instructed Walker to withdraw from the battle before the Chinese could surround the Eighth Army. After the conference at 29 November, Walker ordered all Eighth Army units to retreat to a new line around Sunchon, 48km (30 miles) south of Kunu-ri. The 2nd Infantry Division was one of many forces tasked with covering the retreat. On the morning of 30 November, the 9th Infantry Regiment led the withdrawal by attacking the roadblock. Four tanks were first sent down the road and the PVA held their fire. Encouraged by this development, the 9th Infantry Regiment was ordered to press forward, but PVA machine gun and mortar fire immediately stopped the advance.

ATTACK REPULSED

The ROK 3rd Infantry Regiment attached to the 2nd Infantry Division was sent to reinforce the US 9th Infantry Regiment, but it was routed by friendly fire. With no contacts between the American commands and the British units, the Middlesex Regiment advanced to the south end of the valley without attacking the roadblock. Believing that the roadblock was short, and the British were attacking up the road, the 2nd Infantry Division was ordered to run through the blockade.

As the 2nd Infantry Division entered the valley, the PVA machine guns delivered punishing fire while mortar shells saturated the road. The length of the roadblock caught the 2nd Infantry Division by surprise. The road leading south from Kunu-ri would later be termed 'The Gauntlet', because Chinese soldiers lined the mountains above the narrow road, picking off soldiers and destroying tanks and other vehicles. Here, too, the frigid weather played a vital role in the outcome of the withdrawal.

Eugene Inman fought with the 2nd Infantry Division at the Battle of Kunu-ri. Inman remembered it being so cold that 'rifles and machine guns refused to fire in the low temperatures. The oil in the trucks and jeeps turned to glue, and the vehicles refused to function.' In that particular battle, the cold had led to a wasteland of machinery that had effectively stopped the 2nd Division's escape southward.

Members of the 2nd Infantry that attempted to take cover were promptly

Below: Lt. Gen. Walton H. Walker (left), commander of the Eighth Army, talks with Douglas MacArthur at a conference organized for field commanders in Tokyo, November 1950.

Below: Korean civilians prepare to board an LST during the evacuation of Hungnam, while other refugees transfer some of their meagre belongings from an ox-cart to a fishing boat, December 1950.

left behind by the convoy rushing south, and unit cohesion evaporated. During the day, the air cover tried to suppress the PVA positions with some success, but with no air cover at night, the PVA attack intensified. Finally, the PVA blocked the road completely by destroying the US 38th and 503rd Artillery Battalion of the 2nd Infantry Division, and the immobilized artillery pieces forced the rest of the division to abandon all vehicles and to retreat by hiking through the hills. In one of the last acts of the battle, the 23rd Infantry Regiment fired off its stock of 3206 artillery shells, and the massive barrage shocked the PVA troops from following the regiment. The last stragglers from the US 2nd Infantry Division finally arrived at Sunchon on 1 December, and by 2 December the Eighth Army had completely lost contact with the Chinese.

CHANGJIN RESERVOIR

While the Battle on the Chongchon River marked the start of the Chinese second phase attack in the west, the Changjin Reservoir, a manmade lake located in the northeast of the Korean peninsula, became the site of one of the most brutal campaigns during the Korean War, which included the road that connected Hungnam and the Changjin Reservoir. On 25 November 1950, Chinese forces descended upon the

Eighth Army forces, catching them by surprise and forcing them to retreat. At the same time, Eighth Army forces had been coming in from the west, X Corps was approaching from the east. On 27 November, an X Corps attack proceeded west towards Mupyong, northeast of Kunu, to the rear of Chinese Communist Forces (CCF). The attack called for X Corps, led by the US 1st Marine Division forces commanded by Maj. Gen. Oliver P. Smith, to advance up the west side of the Chosin Reservoir.

The US 7th Infantry, led by Task Force MacLean, advanced along the east side, while the 3rd Infantry Division guarded the Marines' flanks. Trouble quickly ensued, as scattered units of Task Force MacLean were isolated, not only from the rest of the 7th Infantry Division and the Marines but also from each other. To make matters worse, winter had long since descended over the Korean Peninsula, making life at the reservoir harrowing.

Charles McNabb, with B and D Companies, 1st Engineering Battalion, 1st Marine Division, who was posted on the east side of the reservoir at Hagaru-ri, remembers the temperature falling as low as -54°F (-47°C). When recalling the early fighting and the weather, he asserted:

They—the bodies got so high you couldn't shoot over 'em. … You'd set machine guns up on top of bodies. We wasn't dug in. And they got—they started getting bodies. They was froze. You know like it got down to 44 degrees below zero right quick. And later on it got colder than that. Ice would freeze in your nose in 40 degrees and 43. And when you breathe in, ice would freeze. But when it gets down around 50 degrees when you breathe in and breathe out, the ice don't melt. So we cut and stripped some blankets off and legs out of wool underwear and pulled them over our head and had little red goggles we wore. We really needed Arctic, you know, type clothing, but we had mountain sleeping bags. And those sleeping bags, when you got out of one, it'd turn to frost inside, and you start at the bottom, roll it up, try to get the hot air out, you know. The next night when you got in it, it got wet. ... Finally it become useless. It was just wet. They didn't get rid of the frost inside, so we got to wearing the sleeping bag at night with your clothes on.

On 27 November, the X Corps offensive began with the 5th and 7th Marines attacking from Yudam-ni along the west side of Chosin. Two CCF divisions hit the 5th and 7th Marines frontally, while a third cut the road between Yudam-ni and Hagaru-ri. Elements of another division also struck the 7th Infantry. The situation quickly became desperate for the American forces around Chosin. At the same time, Gen. Edward Almond, commander of X Corps, continued to direct the US 7th Infantry up the east side in an attempt to take the Yalu and accomplish MacArthur's goals. Between 27 and 29 November, the battle raged on both sides of the reservoir. Efforts to survive were made possible only by the air support provided by the 1st Marine Air Wing and US Navy Task Force 77.

> EFFORTS TO SURVIVE WERE MADE POSSIBLE ONLY BY THE AIR SUPPORT PROVIDED BY THE 1ST MARINE AIR WING AND US NAVY TASK FORCE 77.

On 30 November, X Corps launched a retreat that would eventually take them south to the port of Hungnam, where they would be transported to the west to aid the Eighth Army. To accomplish that, Task Force Drysdale was ordered from Kot'o-ri to open the road south of Hagaru-ri, where 1st Marine Division headquarters, ammunition dump, and an airfield was located. After a bitter fight, the airfield was opened to traffic by 1 December, allowing UN forces to bring in reinforcements and to evacuate the dead and wounded. After a short rest, UN forces led by the 7th Marines broke out from Hagu-ri and fought their way through Hell Fire Valley, Koto-ri, the Funchilin Pass and Sudong – where Task Force Dog of the 3rd Infantry Division repelled the pursuing PVA 89th Division – and reached the Hungnam perimeter on 11 December.

Between 12 and 24 December, UN forces battled along the perimeter established around the port of Hungnam, while they systematically boarded ships for evacuation to Pusan and Ulsan, a small port 48km (30 miles) north of Pusan. By 24 December, the ships carrying the last X Corps troops and supplies were well out of Hungnam Harbour. They left behind no serviceable equipment or usable supplies and moved to demolish the port once they were safely away.

CHANGES IN THE EIGHTH ARMY

Towards the end of December 1950, UN forces were in full retreat from the surprise Chinese attacks across the Yalu River. If the toll of the engagements from late October until then had not soured the resolve of the retreating UN forces, the death of Eighth US Army commander Walton Walker contributed to the atmosphere of uncertainty.

Walker had drawn the ire of his superior, MacArthur, as he had been critical of the planned UN three-pronged attack towards the Yalu. Walker was aware that the rugged mountainous terrain made mutual support impossible should any of the drives come under serious attack. Complicating things further was the fact that all three drives were spread thin, and were dependent on a long, fragile logistics networks of poor mountain roads that could easily be cut off by a determined enemy.

Prior to the Chinese intervention, MacArthur, with his entourage, flew up from Tokyo to visit Walker and take an aerial tour of the front. During that meeting, MacArthur ordered Walker to maintain an all-out attack. Forced to choose between

Below: US Marines move forward after effective close-air support flushes out the enemy from their hillside entrenchments at Hagaru-ri. Hagaru-ri was the site of the US 1st Marine Division's headquarters, ammunition dump and an airfield.

Above: Pfc. Preston McKnight, of the 19th Infantry Regiment, uses his poncho to get protection from the biting wind and cold, Yoju area, January 1951. Korean winters descended to temperatures of -40°C (-40°F).

an irrational order by his superior and the safety of his men, Walker countermanded his superior and transformed the thrust into a reconnaissance in force based upon frontline intelligence that contradicted MacArthur's assurances of easy victory.

On 25 November, the Chinese entered the war, and Walker had to react to a determined adversary. During those attacks, Walker organized the most difficult of all military manoeuvres – a retreat during battle. His mobile defence during the withdrawal proved so skilful that Walker was able to save most of the Eighth Army. MacArthur, however, was not impressed with him. Never actually liking Walker, MacArthur now found a reason to relieve him of command. Before he could do so, on 23 December 1950, Walker was killed in a traffic accident when a civilian truck collided with his jeep.

Walker's death left a gap in the command structture. He had effectively commanded the Eighth Army from the beginning of its involvement on the Korean peninsula. To replace him, the Army chose Gen. Matthew B. Ridgway, the current deputy chief of staff for administration and training. A successful infantry commander during World War II, Ridgway was keen to mount an attack to turn the tide of the retreat from the Chinese. Upon arriving in Korea, he looked to do just that, but found an Eighth Army defeated in both body and spirit. He took it upon himself to meet the men (from top to bottom), show them that their commander was interested in their fate, and get an honest assessment of the situation. What he found was a completely demoralized force.

Ridgway's surprise did not come only from the lowly enlisted men wose job it was to actually conduct the fighting. He also went to his corps commanders and asked them what their attack plans were. The comanders looked at him in bewilderment and told Ridgway that they had no plan for an attack; they were retreating. These responses precipitated a 'cleaning house' of senior officials in the Eighth Army.

Ridgway was cold and calculating. He did not want ineffective generals who would not or did not possess the capability to command as he sought fit. Much like his friend and mentor George C. Marshall had done in World War II, Ridgway built up a corps of commanders that would heed his orders, motivate their men and stop running. Unfortunately for him, his position was untenable, and he would have to wait to launch his major offensive.

On New Year's Eve, the Chinese and North Koreans attacked with all-out fury. The Eighth Army presented a strong defence, but it wasn't enough. Ridgway later wrote that they 'were killing them by the thousands', but they kept coming. They smashed huge holes in the centre of Ridgway's battle line, where ROK divisions broke and ran. By 2 January, it was evident that the Eighth Army would have to move south of the Han River and abandon Seoul.

Below: Refugees flee southward across the frozen Han River, in advance of Chinese and North Korean communist forces, January 1951. Many displaced North Koreans would never return north after the war, choosing to stay in the Republic where they were offered more freedom.

WONJU

THERE WAS A SERIES of major battles on the UN retreat. Wonju was a critical village set amid the Taebaek Mountains in central Korea. It sat along Route 29, which connected Chuncheon on the 38th Parallel with Daegu on the Pusan Perimeter, a vital line of communication for UN forces. It was also connected to Seoul by another road running northwest that intersected route 29. Its location made it a vital stronghold for the defence of the central and eastern fronts, and was regarded by Eighth Army commander Matthew Ridgway as second only to Seoul in

Below: Allied forces approach Wonju, South Korea, January 1951. Wonju was a critical village set amid the Taebaek Mountains in central Korea and was the site of several battles for control of the 38th Parallel.

order of importance. From 31 December 1950 to 20 January 1951, Wonju was the site of multiple battles that determined who controlled the 38th Parallel and, ultimately, Seoul.

In the First Battle of Wonju, ROK troops found themselves in serious trouble when the People's Volunteer Army forces tasked with cutting the road between Chuncheon and Seoul proved to be too much for them to handle. As part of a greater plan to capture Seoul, the Chinese corps had the ROK troops in a full retreat by the new year, with their retreat route cut off by the Korean People's Army north of Hoengsong.

To break the blockade and open up the path of retreat, the US 2nd Infantry Division and the ROK II Corps conducted an attack from the north and south, forcing a breakthrough by 2 January. Meanwhile, the ROK I Corps had left their original defensive position at Hyon-ri, and North Korean forces flowed in to block the 2nd Division between Wonju and ROK I Corps forces on the coast. Fearing an attempt to surround US forces at Seoul, Ridgway ordered all UN forces to withdraw to the 37th Parallel and establish a new defensive line between Wonju and Chumunjin.

North Korean forces continued to push from the front and east of Wonju, leaving the 2nd Division exposed to the north. Maj. Gen. Edward Almond, commander of US X Corps forces, ordered the 2nd Division to defend the hills surrounding Wonju at all cost. Gen. R.B. McClure, commander of the 2nd Division, felt it would be better to retreat to let UN artillery fire continue to defend Wonju. Unfortunately, he retreated too far for artillery to be effective and Wonju fell to the North Koreans.

Wonju, however, was still deemed vital by Gen. Ridgway, and he ordered the 2nd Division to recapture it the next day. In the following days, the US 23rd and 38th Infantry Regiments, supported by French and Dutch troops, fought in bitterly cold weather against 7000 North Korean soldiers at Hill 247.

North Korean forces prevented UN forces from taking Wonju, but the successful capture of Hill 247 put it within UN artillery range. Although heavy bombardment from UN artillery fire eventually forced the Korean People's Army V Corps to abandon Wonju on 17 January, KPA II Corps had successfully infiltrated the UN rear area, causing a gap between US X Corps forces to the south of Wonju and ROK III Corps forces to the east. Eventually, pressure from roughly 16,000 North Korean guerrilla fighters forced Ridgway to order the 2nd Division to complete a 64-km (40-mile) retreat from Wonju. Ridgway then looked towards launching Operation Thunderbolt against North Korean and Chinese forces, taking the offensive.

THE UN OFFENSIVE

On 20 January 1951, Gen. Ridgway issued a directive designed to convert his current reconnaissance operations into a deliberate counter-attack. Since the enemy situation was still unclear, the action, code-named Operation Thunderbolt, was designed to discover enemy dispositions and intentions with a show of force. The operation had the additional objective of dislodging any enemy forces south of the Han River.

The projected attacks did not represent a full-scale offensive. Phase lines drawn on maps with specific reporting and crossing instructions would be used to tightly control the advance of

the I and IX Corps. The units were to avoid becoming heavily engaged. To accomplish this, each corps would commit only a single US division and ROK regiment. This use of terrain-based phase lines and of limited advances with large forces in reserve was to become the standard procedure for UN offensive operations for the rest of the war.

The first, or western, phase of Operation Thunderbolt lasted from 25 to 31 January. The I and IX Corps moved up 32km (20 miles) into the area south of Seoul. Only the Turkish Brigade, attached to the US 25th Infantry Division, east of Osan, a major city 32km (20 miles) south of Seoul, encountered stiff resistance.

Below: 1 February 1951: following Operation Thunderbolt to dislodge enemy forces along the Han River, troops of the US 35th Infantry Regiment watch for movement as UN forces bombard the area.

Below: This Chinese soldier of the People's Volunteer Army wears a fully quilted jacket and trousers, with archaic puttees. The cap is fur-lined, with extensive earflaps to prevent frostbite. Ammunition for his Type 88 Hanyang rifle is held in cotton bandoliers across the chest.

Elsewhere, opposition was light, with the Chinese merely conducting rearguard actions rather than holding their ground. On 26 January, Suwon, north of Osan, with its large airfield complex, was recaptured. Close air support sorties supported the advance, damaging enemy lines of communication and pounding points of resistance.

As January neared its end, Chinese resistance gradually began to increase, indicating that the main enemy line had almost been reached. On 27 January, the US 3rd Infantry Division joined the attack in the I Corps sector, and on 29 January Ridgway converted Thunderbolt into a full-scale offensive with X Corps joining the offensive on its eastern flank. The I and IX Corps continued a steady, if slow, advance to the Han River against increasingly more vigorous enemy defences. On 2 February, armoured elements of the X Corps reached Wonju. Other elements of the X Corps recaptured Hoengsong, 16km (10 miles) north of Wonju, the same day.

EXPANDED FRONT

While the three US corps advanced west and into the centre, Gen. Ridgway decided to expand the offensive to the east by committing additional elements of the X Corps and the ROK III Corps in an operation code-named Roundup. Roundup's object was the expansion of the offensive to the central sector of the front. The X Corps' ROK 5th and 8th Divisions were to retake Hongch'on, 24km (15 miles) north of Hoengsong, and in the process destroy the North Korean forces in that vicinity. US forces supporting the movement included the 2nd and 7th Infantry Divisions and the 187th Airborne Regimental Combat Team (RCT). Roundup would also protect the right flank of Thunderbolt. Farther east, the ROK III Corps, on X Corps' right flank and still under its control, would also advance north. The operation commenced on 5 February, with both the X and the ROK III Corps attacking steadily, but against increasing enemy resistance.

While UN forces in Operation Thunderbolt advanced to an area just south of the Han against only minor resistance, Chinese and North Korean forces were massing in the central sector north of Hoengsong seeking to renew their offensive south. On the night of 11 February, the enemy struck with five Chinese People's Liberation Army (PLA) armies and two North Korean corps.

The main effort was against X Corps' ROK divisions north of Hoengsong. The Chinese attack, dramatically announced with bugle calls and drum beating, penetrated the ROK line and forced the South Koreans into a ragged withdrawal to the southeast via snow-covered passes in the rugged mountains. The ROK units, particularly the 8th Division, were badly battered in the process, creating large holes in the UN defences. Accordingly, UN forces were soon in a general withdrawal to the south in the central section, giving up most of the terrain recently regained. Despite an attempt to form a solid defensive line, Hoengsong itself was abandoned on 13 February.

On the same day, the Chinese broadened the offensive against the X Corps with attacks against US 2nd Infantry Division positions near Chip'yong-ni. They also attacked further to the west out of a bridgehead south of the Han near Yangp'yong against elements of the US 24th Infantry Division. The 21st Infantry of the 24th Division quickly contained the Yangp'yong attack that was aimed towards Suwon, but at Chip'yong-ni the Chinese encircled the 2nd Division's 23rd Infantry and its attached French Army battalion, cleverly exploiting a gap in

Above: February 1951: three US soldiers rest on a snowy hillside after successfully assaulting enemy positions as part of Operation Roundup, which expanded the offensive to the central sector north of Hoengsong.

ASSAULT ON HILL 180

As part of the I Corps attack, the US 25th Infantry Division advanced against stiff enemy resistance in high ground south of Seoul. One obstacle, Hill 180, an enemy strongpoint located near Soam-ni, proved particularly difficult. In the resulting hand-to-hand combat, the American shock action carried the day, routing the enemy from well-entrenched positions atop the hill. The surviving defenders fled the battlefield, leaving their equipment and weapons behind. On 9 February, the enemy defence opposite I and IX Corps gave way. Soon, UN units in the west were racing northward. The US 25th Infantry Division retook Inch'on and Kimpo Airfield as elements of I Corps closed on the south bank of the Han opposite Seoul.

the overextended American lines. Chip'yong-ni was deemed strategically important because of its location along the Han River. From 13–15 February, the Chinese concentrated their focus on Chip'yong-ni. Although the 23rd Infantry held on at Chip'yong-ni, the situation to the southeast was grave.

At the time, Ridgway and Almond were seeking to stabilize the front line between Chip'yong-ni and Wonju, where the destruction of the ROK forces around Hoengsong had created major gaps in the defensive line. For three desperate days, the front wavered as the Chinese attempted to exploit these gaps before UN reinforcements could arrive. Ridgway quickly pushed units into the critical areas, moving the 27th British Commonwealth Brigade and the ROK 6th Division over to X Corps and into the gap south of Chip'yong-ni. The action proved timely. On the night of 13–14 February, the Chinese conducted major assaults at Chip'yong-ni, Ch'uam-ni, 8km (5 miles) southeast of Chip'yong-ni, and at Wonju. Supported by massed artillery and air support, the UN forces repulsed the attacks, causing heavy Chinese casualties.

Elsewhere on 15 February, efforts to restore the front were finally realized. Rather than take advantage of the weakened front to the east, the Chinese had chosen to concentrate on eliminating the US forces at Chip'yong-ni first. But they had chosen poorly, and the respite allowed UN forces to restore their lines. Reinforcements, particularly the US 7th Infantry Division and 187th Airborne RCT, helped the South Koreans form a solid line around Wonju and near Chech'on.

By 18 February, the communist offensive was spent, and enemy forces began withdrawing to the north rather than attempting to hold what they had taken. With the enemy withdrawing, Ridgway ordered IX Corps to advance, while the X Corps moved to destroy the communist forces around Chech'on in the central sector. With the initiative restored and fully in the hands of the UN forces by 19 February, Ridgway ordered the commencement of Operation Killer (20 February–6 March 1951), the UN counteroffensive.

OPERATION RIPPER

On 7 March, Ripper began with I and IX Corps on the west near Seoul and Hoengsong and X and ROK III Corps in the east.

Below: A US 1st Division Sherman tank drives north through Chuncheon, South Korea, March 1951.

On the left, the US 25th Infantry Division quickly crossed the Han and established a bridgehead. Farther to the east, IX Corps reached its first phase line on 11 March. Three days later, the advance proceeded to the next phase line. During the night of 14 March, elements of the ROK 1st Division and US 3rd Infantry Division liberated Seoul. The capital city changed hands for the fourth and last time in the war. The communist forces were compelled to abandon it when the UN approach to the east of the city threatened the defenders with encirclement.

UN forces continued to meet their objectives, pushing the enemy further back across the 38th Parallel in subsequent operations named Courageous, Rugged and Dauntless. During Operation Rugged, designed to secure a new line, 'Kansas', just north of the 38th Parallel, a major change in the Far East Command and, as a result, the United Nations Command, took place on 11 April.

President Truman and Eighth Army commander Matthew Ridgway wanted to press the Chinese and North Korean troops out of South Korea. Once

Below: MacArthur inspects troops of the 24th Infantry Regiment on his arrival at Kimpo airfield for a tour of the battlefront, February 1951.

OPERATION KILLER

OPERATION KILLER WAS DESIGNED to enhance the damage to enemy forces in a methodical manner. Ridgway named the operation as such, in the hopes that it would ignite an offensive spirit in the Eighth Army and continue the momentum gained hitherto. The IX, X and ROK III Corps were directed north towards a line named 'Arizona' running from Yangp'yong east to positions north of Hoengsong and along the east–west portion of the Wonju–Kangnung highway. By 28 February, all of the units involved had met their goals, pushing their lines forward 19–24km (12–15 miles). Once the objectives of Killer were met, Ridgway, with the support of MacArthur, commenced Operation Ripper, which envisioned the recapture of Seoul and the towns of Hongch'on, 80km (50 miles) west of Seoul, and Ch'unch'on, 24km (15 miles) further north.

Left: Men of the US 1st Marine Division capture Chinese troops during fighting on the central front, Hoengsong, March 1951.

they were successfully routed north, however, Truman wanted to establish a negotiated peace with the enemy. Gen. MacArthur, commander of FECOM and UNC, did not feel the same. He wanted to expand the war against China and frequently complained that the president was tying his hands by forbidding the bombing of China, thereby sacrificing American lives and endangering American freedom.

Truman prepared a statement to establish a ceasefire. On 20 March, the Joint Chiefs of Staff made MacArthur aware of the impending statement. As commander of all forces in the region, it made sense that he be updated so he could incorporate the information into his plans in theatre. MacArthur was keenly aware of how the desires of the president would affect his ability to plan future operations. On 23 March, MacArthur issued the following communiqué about offering a ceasefire to the Chinese.

> *Of even greater significance than our tactical successes has been the clear revelation that this new enemy, Red China, of such exaggerated and vaunted military power, lacks the industrial capability to provide adequately many critical items necessary to the conduct of modern war. He lacks the manufacturing base and those raw materials needed to produce, maintain and operate even moderate air and naval power, and he cannot provide the essentials for successful ground operations, such as tanks, heavy artillery and other refinements science has introduced into the conduct of military campaigns. Formerly his great numerical potential might well have filled this gap but with the development of existing methods of mass destruction numbers alone do not offset the vulnerability inherent in such deficiencies.*
>
> *...*
>
> *These military weaknesses have been clearly and definitely revealed since Red China entered upon its undeclared war in Korea. Even under the inhibitions which now restrict the activity of the United Nations forces and the corresponding military advantages which accrue to Red China, it has been shown its complete inability to accomplish by force of arms the conquest of Korea. The enemy, therefore must by now be painfully aware that a decision of the United Nations to depart from its tolerant effort to contain the war to the area of Korea, through an expansion of our military operations to its coastal areas and interior bases, would doom Red China to the risk of imminent military collapse. These basic facts being established, there should be no insuperable difficulty in arriving at decisions on the Korean problem if the issues are*

> MACARTHUR WAS KEENLY AWARE OF HOW THE DESIRES OF THE PRESIDENT WOULD AFFECT HIS ABILITY TO PLAN FUTURE OPERATIONS.

Opposite: 23 March 1951: Fairchild C-119s drop paratroopers of the 187th RCT to cut off retreating enemy units south of Munsan, as part of Operation Ripper.

Above: General Matthew B. Ridgway (foreground) and General James A. Van Fleet assessing the situation. Ridgway took over as Commander-in-Chief of UN forces after MacArthur was fired, and Van Fleet replaced Ridgway as commander of the Eighth US Army.

resolved on their own merits, without being burdened by extraneous matters not directly related to Korea, such as Formosa or China's seat in the United Nations.

MACARTHUR LEAVES

The day after he issued the communiqué, MacArthur authorized Ridgway to advance up to 32km (20 miles) north of the 38th Parallel. Truman was furious. He and MacArthur had been at odds before, but he viewed MacArthur's actions in this case as a direct violation of the directives he had discussed with him at their Wake Island meeting the previous December. He believed MacArthur's communiqué to be far 'beyond the scope and place of a military commander of the United Nations to issue on his own responsibility. It was an act totally disregarding all directives to abstain from any declarations on foreign policy. It was in open defiance of my orders as President and as Commander-in-Chief. This was a challenge to the authority of the President under the Constitution. It also flouted the policy of the United Nations.'

When MacArthur gave approval for Operation Rugged, to pursue the enemy north of the 38th Parallel, Truman held a meeting in his office with Averell Harriman, his special secretary, Secretary of Defense George C. Marshall, Chairman of the JCS Omar Bradley, and Secretary of State Dean Acheson to discuss what would be done about MacArthur. With a unanimous decision among the attendees reached, President Truman relieved MacArthur of command on 11 April and replaced him with Eighth Army Commander Matthew Ridgway. Ridgway in turn was replaced as Eighth Army commander by Lt. Gen. James Van Fleet. He continued Ridgway's policy of using coordinated firepower, rolling with communist counterpunches, and inflicting maximum casualties.

PHILIPPINE EXPEDITIONARY FORCES TO KOREA

The Philippine Expeditionary Forces arrived in Korea in August 1950. It was composed of 1468 troops and was the fifth-largest force under the United Nations Command. During 22–23 April 1951 at the Battle of Yultong, the Filipino 10th Battalion Combat Team (BCT), who were part of the 65th Infantry Regiment, battled the Chinese PVA 44th Division. Although the 10th BCT became trapped and lost all contact with the outside world, the Filipinos held their position until the Chinese stopped their attacks on the morning of 23 April. The 10th BCT's action at Yultong allowed the US 3rd Infantry Division to successfully withdraw from the battlefield and later turned the tide of the Korean War.

By the time Van Fleet took control of the Eighth Army, Operation Rugged was underway. I and IX Corps had moved forward towards Ch'orwon, southwest of the Iron Triangle, and reached an intermediate phase line, Utah. To their right, X Corps forces took a dam overlooking the Hwach'on Reservoir five days later. On 20 April, the last UN forces, the US 7th Infantry Division and the ROK 3rd Division of the X Corps, reached the Kansas line. Final preparations began to continue the advance to the Wyoming line. However, all UN offensive action ceased when communist forces launched their spring offensive across the entire front.

THE CHINESE SPRING OFFENSIVE

The Chinese Spring Offensive, also known as the Chinese Fifth Phase Campaign, was designed by the Chinese to destroy US I and IX Corps above the Han River. General Peng Dehuai, the commander-in-chief of the Chinese and North Korean communist forces in the field, promised the capture of Seoul as a May Day gift to Mao Zedong. He planned to 'wipe out... the American 3rd Division... the British 27th Brigade and the 1st

> WITH A UNANIMOUS DECISION AMONG THE ATTENDEES REACHED, PRESIDENT TRUMAN RELIEVED MACARTHUR OF COMMAND ON 11 APRIL.

Division of the Puppet Army... and then American 24th Division and 25th Division.'

At his disposal were three Chinese army groups – the 3rd, 9th and 19th Army Groups – and three North Korean corps – the I, III and V Corps. The offensive commenced on 22 April on two broad fronts: the main thrust across the Imjin River in the western sector held by the US I Corps involved 337,000 troops driving towards Seoul, while the secondary effort involved 149,000 troops attacking further east across the Soyang River in the central and eastern sectors, falling primarily on the US IX Corps, and to a lesser extent on the US X Corps sector.

A further 214,000 Chinese troops supported the offensive; in total, more than 700,000 men. As part of the preparation, the battle-hardened 39th and 40th Armies of the 13th Army Group were transferred to the 9th Army Group under the overall command of Song Shi-Lun, and Commander Wen Yuchen of the

Below: A Chinese patrol tries to dislodge South Korean soldiers from a shelter built on a rocky hill as part of their Spring Offensive.

CHINESE INTERVENTION

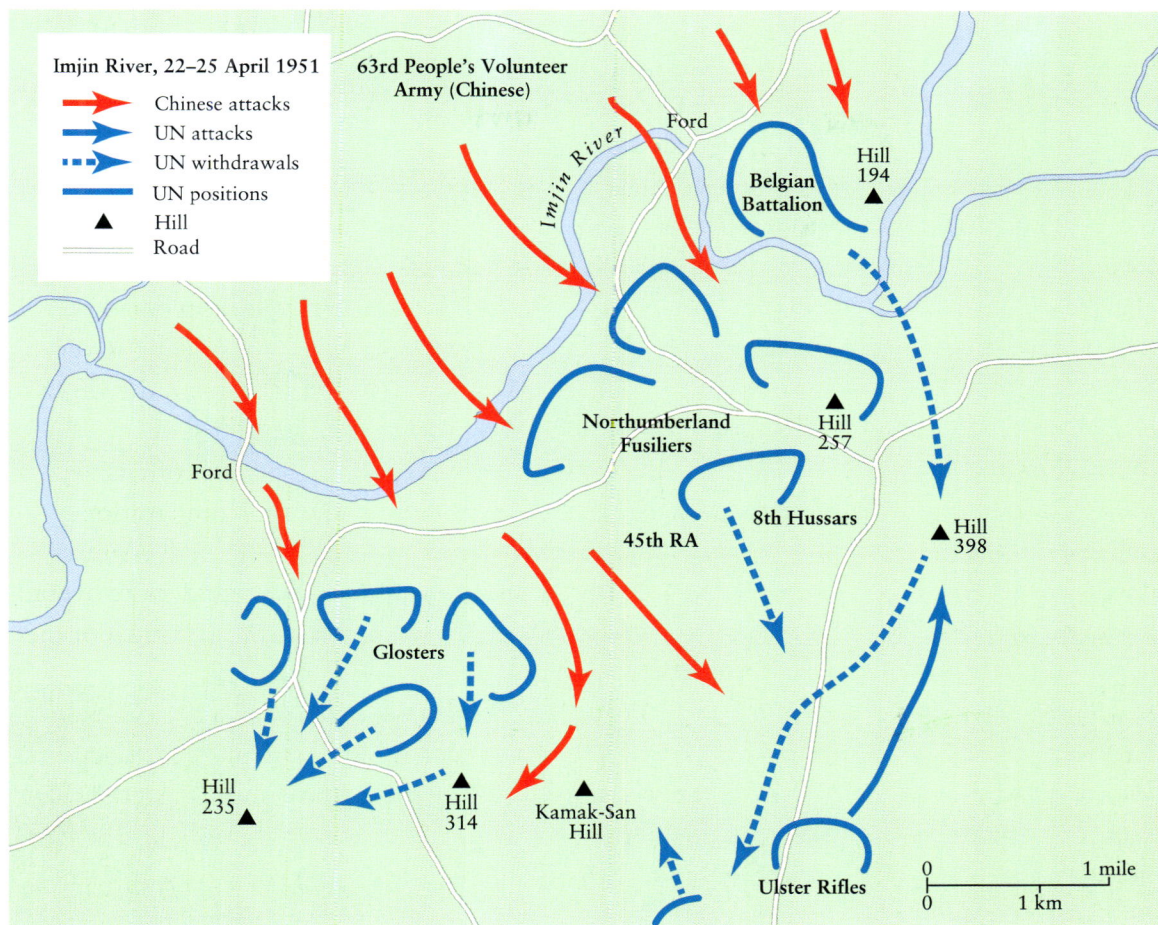

40th Army was given the mission of destroying the South Korean 6th Division while blocking any UN reinforcements towards the Imjin River at Kapyong.

BATTLE OF THE IMJIN RIVER

The first offensive of this campaign commenced on 22 April, when the Chinese attacked the UN forces at the south bank of the Imjin River, a strategically crucial location heading a historic invasion route to Seoul. The section of the UN line where the battle took place was defended primarily by British forces of the 29th Infantry Brigade, consisting of three British and one Belgian infantry battalion supported by tanks and artillery. Despite facing a numerically superior enemy, the brigade held its positions for

Above: At Imjin River, Chinese forces attempted to breakthrough in their push to recapture Seoul. The area was defended by the 29th Infantry Brigade, made up of three British and one Belgian infantry battalions. Their actions slowed the Chinese advance and allowed defensive positions to be established north of Seoul.

16TH FIELD REGIMENT, ROYAL NEW ZEALAND ARTILLERY

THIS REGIMENT ARRIVED IN Korea on New Year's Eve 1950 and joined the British 27th Infantry Brigade on 21 January 1951. The New Zealanders immediately saw combat and spent the next two and a half years taking part in the operations, most notably the Battle of Kapyong and the First Battle of Maryang San, which led the United Nations forces back to and over the 38th Parallel.

Below: An M24 Chaffee used by the 79th Tank Battalion, 25th Infantry Division, in Operation Ripper, where the enemy were driven across the Han River. Success continued with Operations Dauntless, Detonate and Piledriver in the Spring of 1951. These offensives enhanced the UN's bargaining platform.

three days, repelling several human wave attacks and inflicting more than 10,000 casualties in the process. After being encircled, however, the 1st Battalion Gloucestershire Regiment, nicknamed the 'Glosters', was nearly destroyed and those who survived were captured.

When the units of the 29th Infantry Brigade were ultimately forced to fall back, supported by the defensive rearguard actions of the Filipino contingent during the Battle of Yultong, their actions in the Battle of the Imjin River, together with those of other UN forces, had blunted the impetus of the Chinese offensive and allowed UN forces to retreat to prepared defensive positions in the area called the 'No-Name Line' just 8km (5 miles) north of Seoul, where the Chinese were halted. Both sides then realized that the prospect of the communists parading along the streets of Seoul during May Day had evaporated. On the other hand, although the UN forces made a strategic gain during the battle by preventing the Chinese from recapturing Seoul, the loss of the unit caused much controversy in Britain and within the UN Command.

KAPYONG VALLEY AND SOYANG RIVER

In the Kapyong sector of the offensive, the 27th British Commonwealth Brigade established blocking positions in the Kapyong Valley, also one of the key routes south to the capital, Seoul. The two forward battalions, 3rd Battalion, Royal Australian Regiment (3 RAR) and 2nd Battalion, Princess Patricia's Canadian Light Infantry (2 PPCLI), occupied positions astride the valley and hastily developed defences on 23 April.

Above: British soldiers of the 1st Battalion, the Gloucestershire Regiment, ride atop their Universal Carrier after fighting their way out of a communist encirclement, May 1951.

As thousands of South Korean soldiers began to withdraw through the valley, the Chinese infiltrated the brigade position under the cover of darkness and assaulted the Australians on Hill 504 during the evening and into the following day. Although heavily outnumbered, the 27th Brigade held their positions into the afternoon before the Australians withdrew to positions to the rear of the brigade on the evening of 24 April, with both sides having suffered heavy casualties. The Chinese then turned their attention to the Canadians on Hill 677, but during a fierce night battle they were unable to dislodge them.

The fighting helped stem the Chinese offensive, and the actions of the Australians and Canadians at Kapyong were important in helping to prevent a breakthrough on the United Nations Command central front. The two battalions bore the brunt of the assault and stopped an entire Chinese division during the hard-fought battle. The next day, the Chinese withdrew back up the valley to the north, in order to regroup for the second impulse of the offensive.

The second offensive occurred at the Battle of the Soyang River. Even though the communist forces lost the strategic initiative after the first offensive, Mao insisted that the second phase of the offensive still be carried out. The attack took place across the entire front, but with the main thrust below the Soyang River in the Taebaek Mountains. The objective of the main effort was to sever the six Republic of Korea Army (ROKA) divisions on the eastern front from the remainder of the Eighth US Army and annihilate them and the US 2nd Infantry Division.

The attack was launched on 16 May and succeeded in swiftly pushing back the ROKA I Corps, which retreated in good order, and III Corps, which was routed, while the US 2nd Infantry Division to their left mounted a stronger defence before gradually giving up ground. Elements of the US 2nd Infantry, ROKA I Corps, ROKA III Corps, a French battalion and a Netherlands battalion eventually prevailed with the support of UN air and artillery strikes.

Although the Chinese Spring Offensive was a costly engagement for UN units, they succeeded in preventing the capture of Seoul. The fighting had blunted the Chinese offensive, causing it to lose momentum, and allowed UN forces in the area to withdraw to the No-Name Line, a defensible position north of Seoul. Despite their numerical advantage, the Chinese had been badly outgunned, and they could not overcome the well-trained and well-armed UN forces. The battlefield was littered with the corpses of Chinese soldiers, a testament to the discipline and

Below: Marines take cover behind an M26 tank while it fires on enemy positions ahead. Hongchon Area, 22 May 1951.

2ND BATTALION, PRINCESS PATRICIA'S CANADIAN LIGHT INFANTRY

ON 15 AUGUST 1950, the 2nd Battalion was created within Princess Patricia's Canadian Light Infantry (PPCLI) as a component of the Canadian Army Special Force in response to the North Korean invasion of South Korea. On 21 February 1951, the 2 PPCLI was involved in Operation Killer, a counter-offensive by the United Nations forces to push communist Chinese and North Korean armies back behind the Han River and recover the South Korean capital. The 2 PPCLI's goal was to advance towards Hill 404. On their way, they were flanked on both sides but managed to continue up the hill to have the high ground.

On 21 February, the Patricias left the small village of Sangsok and headed north to their assigned objective of a new hill called Hill 419. This hill was defended by the Chinese. The Patricias D Company led by Capt. J.G. Turnbull were to attack, but the ridge of the hill gave an easy line of sight for the Chinese. The Canadians took fire from every direction from cannons, rockets and small arms fire. They were under intense fire. Their attack was postponed for 36 hours, but they kept up aggressive patrols

Above: Private Morris J. Piche is helped to an aid station in the Kapyong Valley by Lance Corporal W.J. Chrysler. Both men were from the 2nd Battalion, Princess Patricia's Canadian Light Infantry.

and eventually the Australians gained control of Hill 619. The Australians taking Hill 619 made the Chinese leave Hill 419 and the Canadians took that hill without serious opposition.

firepower of the defenders. And yet, despite their ultimate defeat, the battle once again demonstrated that the Chinese were tough and skilful soldiers capable of inflicting heavy casualties.

THE FINAL UN COUNTER-ATTACK

On 18 May, in response to the Chinese Spring Offensive, UN commander Gen. Matthew Ridgway suggested to Eighth US Army commander Gen. James Van Fleet that he should attempt to relieve the pressure on his forces in the east by attacking in the west to threaten enemy lines of communication in the Iron Triangle. Ridgway recommended a two-division attack moving on the Route 33 axis towards Ch'orwon. Using intelligence that suggested pervasive low morale among the Chinese forces and their clearly overextended position, Ridgway enlarged his concept the following day to take advantage of their vulnerability and ordered Van Fleet to attack across the entire front. Agreeing that the PVA/KPA forces could be trapped, Van Fleet laid out an operation that he believed could produce decisive results if the attack moved fast enough.

Below: Navy corpsmen prepare three wounded US Marines for evacuation via helicopter at Kari San Mountain, May 1951.

Van Fleet's plan called for I Corps, IX Corps and part of the 1st Marine Division at the left of X Corps to advance on 20 May towards the Munsan-Chuncheon segment of Line Topeka, 24km (15 miles) north of the defences at Seoul. Once the Topeka segment was occupied, strikes to start closing the noose were to be made towards the Iron Triangle – one up Route 3 to secure a road centre in the Yongp'yong River valley some 32km (20 miles) above Uijongbu; another up Route 17 beyond Chuncheon to seize the complex of road junctions at the west end of the Hwacheon Reservoir.

Within a week, UN forces had successfully routed the enemy at these locations, on the Syuoang River bridge, Kansong. By 27 May, they had reached their objectives but had allowed most major Chinese units to escape entrapment. To extend the reach of the UN counter-attack, Van Fleet ordered Operation Piledriver.

In the west, I and IX Corps were to seize Line Wyoming to cut PVA/KPA lines of communication at the base of the Iron Triangle and to block the main roads running southeast out of the triangle towards the Hwacheon Reservoir and Chuncheon.

The weight of the western attack was to be in the I Corps zone. Reinforced by the 3rd Division and its attached ROKA 9th Division, and backed up by the 187th Airborne Regimental Combat Team, I and IX Corps were to seize the Ch'orwon-Kumhwa area. In a narrowed IX Corps zone, the ground beyond Hwacheon town was to be taken to block the roads reaching southeast out of Kumhwa.

East of the reservoir, after completing operations to capture the Yanggu-Inje area and reach Kansong on the east coast, X Corps and ROKA I Corps were to seize and establish defensive positions along a newly drawn segment of Line Kansas running northeast from the reservoir across the southern rim of a hollow circle of mountains aptly called the 'Punchbowl' to the coastal town of Kojin-ni 8km (5 miles) above Kansong. Once on the adjusted line, both Corps could use the road as their main supply route and, in addition, could receive supplies through the port at Kansong. Van Fleet had in mind another use for Kansong as part of an operation that he planned to open on 6 June to isolate and destroy PVA/KPA forces that had succeeded in withdrawing above Route 24 into the area northeast of the Hwacheon Reservoir, but Ridgway did not feel the gains would be worth the risks.

LIMITED OFFENSIVE

Ridgway did approve the preceding two plans, and when the Eighth Army seized Line Wyoming and the adjusted segment of Line Kansas in the east, it had reached its allowed limit of general advance in support of efforts to open ceasefire negotiations. As yet, there had been no clear sign that Chinese and North Korean authorities favoured that kind of resolution, but there had been a search for a way to open armistice talks.

> RIDGWAY AGREED THAT LINE KANSAS WOULD BE THE BEST LOCATION FOR THE EIGHTH ARMY IF ARMISTICE NEGOTIATIONS STARTED SOON.

On 9 June, Van Fleet offered Ridgway several plans for limited offensive action to keep PVA/KPA forces off balance, three of which he proposed to execute immediately after the Eighth Army reached Lines Kansas and Wyoming. Each of the three called for a raid on enemy troops and supplies within a specific area. In the west, a division was to hit Kaesong 16km (10 miles) above the Imjin River. In the central region, an armoured task force was to attack P'yonggang at the apex of the Iron Triangle, and the 1st Marine Division was to make an amphibious landing at T'ongch'on and attack southwest over Route 17 to join Eighth Army lines at Kumhwa.

Ridgway agreed with Van Fleet's concept of holding the Eighth Army along the Kansas–Wyoming front and punishing enemy forces with limited attacks, but refused the 1st Marine Division operation, presumably for the same reasons that he had refused Van Fleet's earlier T'ongch'on landing proposal. He approved the other attack plans, but they were to be executed only if intelligence confirmed that worthwhile targets existed in the Kaesong and P'yonggang areas.

Ridgway then requested recommendations on the best location for the Eighth Army during a ceasefire. Van Fleet recommended Line Kansas because of its suitability for a strong defence, but pointed out that since a ceasefire agreement might require opposing forces to withdraw several miles from the line of contact to create a buffer zone, the Eighth Army would have to be well forward of Line Kansas at the time an agreement was reached. Ridgway agreed that Line Kansas would be the best location for the Eighth Army if armistice negotiations started soon. He assured Van Fleet that, if possible, he would advise him of forthcoming negotiations in time to allow him to move at least part of his forces to a line of contact 32km (20 miles) above Kansas.

So ended the period of the Korean War characterized by main offensives. The rest of the war would be characterized as a stalemate. Fighting still continued, but was conducted for limited aims, and never reached the scale of the offensives that characterized the first year of the war.

Below: Pfc. Roman Prauty (crouching foreground) and his gun crew of 31st RCT, fires a 75mm (2.95in) recoilless rifle in support of infantry units across the valley near Oetlook-tong, June 1951.

4

THE WAR IN THE AIR

The 1950–53 Korean War is unique with respect to airpower because most of the aerial combat that occurred was between Russian and American pilots rather than among the Koreans. While the Korean War as a whole has become known as the 'Forgotten War', the air war on both sides of the 38th Parallel inflicted irrevocable damage on the landscape and on the psyches of those who bore witness to it.

IN HIS work on the Korean War, historian Brian Cummings notes that the American-led air war punished North Korea for three years without regard to civilian casualties. Air assaults ranged from the widespread use of firebombing to the threatened use of nuclear and chemical weapons. Although Cummings' research is geared towards the memory of the war in a Korean context, the fact remains that the Allied air effort resembled the annihilationist strategies employed in World War II. That in itself is interesting when the espoused strategy was to engage in a limited campaign with clear rules of engagement designed not to escalate into a 'hot' war with the Soviet Union.

Opposite: Five North American F-86A Sabre fighters of the 4th Fighter Interceptor Wing on the flight line at Suwon, June 1951. The Sabre was one of the new jet-propelled fighters used in the Korean War.

The history of the air war in Korea between 1950 and 1953 could fill a book-length study on its own, but there are a number of topics that are important precursors to such a study, as is a discussion of those who actually fought in the air war. The UN force predominantly comprised US air elements, so the following analysis will support that fact, but other contributors to the air war effort will also be addressed.

SUWON AIRFIELD

The first use of UN air power, predominantly made up of US forces, was on Kimpo Airfield and Suwon Airfield on 27 June 1950. When the war began two days earlier with the North Korean invasion, US forces attempted to evacuate US civilians and diplomats from the city of Seoul, where a battle was ongoing between North and South Korean forces. Transport aircraft and ships, escorted by US fighter planes, attempted to take civilians out of the country as fast as possible. During these missions on 27 June, US forces were attacked by North Korean aircraft in two separate incidents in the Seoul area. Despite being outnumbered, the better-built American aircraft outmanoeuvred

Below: July 1950: a tea shop in Suwon puts up a welcome sign for US servicemen. Suwon Airfield was one of the first and most vital airfields captured on the Korean peninsula at the start of the war.

the North Koreans, quickly shooting down half of the attacking force.

The air battle over Suwon was important for numerous reasons. For one, US forces emerged victorious after being first attacked by North Korean forces. Secondly, it marked the first engagement of the newly constituted United States Air Force (USAF). The most important reason, however, was its place as the turning point from conventional fighters to those powered by jet engines. The fight pitted the US P-51 Mustang and the F-80C Shooting Star, the first jet-powered plane used by the USAF, against the North Korean Lavochkin La-7 and Ilyushin Il-10. While the Korean People's Air Force (KPAF) attacked first, the F-80 aircraft were able to attack the North Koreans from a greater distance and had far better manoeuvrability. The Ilyushin Il-10 was considered formidable in World War II, but it failed in comparison to the new jet-powered planes. The discrepancy in the air technology and the early Allied victory at Suwon gave the North Koreans pause when planning any future air campaigns.

Above: A Russian-made Ilyushin ground attack aircraft stands at Kimpo Airfield after being strafed and rocketed by United Nation's aircraft. Dubbed the 'flying tank', the Il-2 and Il-10 models enjoyed great success before the use of jet-propelled aircraft.

CLOSE AIR SUPPORT

Although the move to jet-powered planes was effective, so too was the use of airplanes as close support for ground forces. It was not a new concept, and indeed the main purpose for airplanes in Korea was just that: to support the major ground elements. Air elements in all US forces (Army Air Corps, Navy and Marines) had started training for the use of planes in support roles, but the Marine Corps was the only service that specifically trained its pilots to carry out such missions. The use of aircraft in support of ground units had been the heart of marine aviation since its

P-51 MUSTANG

This World War II veteran was considered the best long-range ground-attack aircraft in Far East Command by General Stratemeyer, commander of the Far East Air Forces. It was fitted with rockets and bombs, and photo reconnaissance, rather than operating in the pure fighter-interceptor role. After the first North Korean invasion, USAF units were forced to fly from bases in Japan; the F-51Ds, with their long range and endurance, could attack targets in Korea that short-ranged F-80 jets could not. Because of their vulnerable liquid cooling system, however, the P-51s sustained heavy losses to ground fire.

Above: A P-51D Mustang fighter used by the South African Air Force (SAAF) that served with the 18th Fighter-Bomber Wing, USAF, prepares to take off, May 1951.

inception in 1912. Effective close air support had been hampered by limits in communication, aircraft, ordnance, and command and control. In World War II, all military services made significant strides towards accomplishing genuinely effective close air support. The severe military cutbacks subsequent to World War II revealed the true commitment of each service to close air support. In this environment, the Marine Corps put its confidence in close air support and worked to improve capabilities in using aircraft in support of infantry Marines.

The Marines were the only service that used a ground coordinator, later known as a forward air controller (FAC). They provided their FACs with an exceptional level of authority. FACs served as agents of the ground commanders, usually posted at the battalion level. As such, they had direct tactical control over the prosecution of the air strike. They could determine the level of air support needed and then brief the pilot on how the strike was to be conducted.

The Marine Corps validated and legitimized the FAC role by ensuring that first-rate pilots served in those billets and, indeed, even made serving as an FAC a career-enhancing experience. The small size of Marine aviation ensured that the FACs and the pilots overhead often knew one another personally and, because they spoke the same language, air support was enhanced. Furthermore, assigning aviators to FAC roles spurred a multidisciplinary attitude that enhanced better air–ground integration.

In previous wars, air–ground support had not been the priority. In the latter stages of World War II, naval airpower existed to protect the fleet. In Korea, with the Seventh Fleet having control over the Strait of Formosa and remaining uncontested in the waters off Korea, US and UN forces could focus more on the land war and the use of airpower for ground support. Close air support in Korea for US forces followed the Joint Training Directive for Air–Ground Operations (JTD). The US commander of Far East Air Forces (FEAF) was Lt. Gen. George E. Stratemeyer. At the start of the Korean War, his forces were an occupation force, and its charter was the air defence of its area of operations, which included Japan, the Ryukyus, the Marianas and the Philippines. It had many secondary missions, including air support of operations as arranged with

Below: Lieutenant General George Stratemeyer (right), commander of the Far East Air Forces, awards Royal Air Force Wing Commander Peter Wykeham-Barnes the distinguished US Air Medal for service in Korea.

appropriate Army and Navy commanders. Little training, however, had been accomplished with the Army because of the severe budget cuts that followed World War II.

During the early, desperate days of the war, Stratemeyer and his vice commander, Maj. Gen. Otto P. Weyland, tried their best to provide the ground forces with needed support, using B-26s, B-29s and even F-82s for close air support. Although many ground commanders appreciated the support given them by FEAF aircraft, notably the 2nd Infantry Division during the ordeal in its battle south of Kunu-ri in early December 1950, others did not. World War II had shown that close air support worked best in fluid situations, when the enemy was on the move. In the static conditions that occurred during the last two years of the Korean War, when the enemy was dug in deeply, artillery fire was often a better choice than air.

IN THE STATIC CONDITIONS OF THE LAST TWO YEARS OF THE KOREAN WAR, WHEN THE ENEMY WAS DUG IN DEEPLY, ARTILLERY FIRE WAS OFTEN A BETTER CHOICE THAN AIR.

Unfortunately, the ground troops had become used to having air support virtually on-call, and they were not pleased when the airmen began to seek more lucrative targets behind the lines – in other words, interdiction. More instances of friendly fire occurred during the static phase of the war as well. Commanders on the ground noted that they could always get air support when needed, but their ability to hit stationary enemy forces was not the best.

INTERDICTION

The interdiction effort had three discernible phases – two distinguishable by a difference in principal target, the other by its concept of attack. In Phase I, which lasted from August to November 1950, selected rail and highway bridges were the principal targets. Until mid-September, the bridge targets were located variously from southwestern Korea to the Yalu River boundary between Korea and Manchuria.

It was the FEAF concept that destroying the main bridges in North Korea would sever enemy road and rail traffic from the north and that concurrent attacks on river crossings in South

Opposite: The lead B-29 bomber of the 19th Bomb Group of the United States Air Force carries out its 150th combat mission in Korea, February 1951.

Korea would interdict the flow of enemy troops and materiel to the battlefront. In September and October, as UN troops pushed the North Koreans out of South Korea and moved above the 38th Parallel, FEAF concentrated on bridges whose destruction could help to prevent an orderly retreat by the North Koreans.

Then, when the Chinese first appeared in Korea in late October and early November, seven interdictory air attacks centred on the international road and rail bridges spanning the Yalu. In Phase II, from December 1950 to August 1951, bridges were again the main targets, but emphasis was placed on concentrated attacks within designated zones. The zones received priorities according to their considered importance to enemy movements, and the air plan called for attacks by massed airpower, one zone at a time, according to the established priorities. Special attention was given to the rail system since the enemy was expected to make maximum use of its larger capacity.

As a result, the enemy shifted the bulk of its movements from the rail lines to the road. Consequently, near the end of Phase II, the area destruction plan was modified to include concentrated attacks on major roads within a specified zone. Beginning in June 1951, this effort, known as Operation Strangle, concentrated on the roads in a one-degree latitudinal belt across the peninsula just above the battle line. This operation lasted for two months and bridged Phases II and III.

In Phase III, which lasted for ten months from August 1951 to June 1952, the rail system became the principal target. Whereas previous operations against rail lines had stressed the destruction of bridges, the new

Below: The shattered remnants of the Wonsan petroleum refinery after B-29 bomber strikes are used to destroy North Korean industrial capacity, August 1950.

objective was to make multiple cuts of the tracks and roadbeds. Repairing such damage, it was judged, would be more difficult for the enemy than repairing or replacing downed bridge spans.

At the termination of this effort, a program of general destruction was instituted wherein all available airpower was employed to make the conflict as costly as possible to the enemy in terms of equipment, facilities and personnel. Although this might be considered a fourth interdictory phase, interdiction itself became secondary to the intended purpose of encouraging the Chinese and North Koreans to conclude armistice negotiations. This new period is often referred to as the 'air pressure'.

AIR PRESSURE

As the stalemate on the ground and the ineffectiveness of air interdiction continued amid truce negotiations in 1952, the FEAF looked for more effective means to use air power to force the North Koreans to quit the war. A US Air Staff Study of 1952 recommended that any air resources beyond those required to maintain air superiority be employed towards accomplishing the maximum amount of selected destruction, thus making the Korean conflict as costly as possible to the enemy in terms of equipment, supplies and personnel. Targets were prioritized on the basis of the effect their destruction would have on the enemy, their vulnerability to available weapons, and the cost to FEAF of attacking them.

> TARGETS WERE PRIORITIZED ON THE BASIS OF THE EFFECT THEIR DESTRUCTION WOULD HAVE ON THE ENEMY.

Suggested objectives included hydroelectric plants, locomotives and vehicles, stored supplies, and even buildings in cities and villages, especially in areas that were active in support of enemy forces. Based on the study, interdiction was to be abandoned to concentrate on the new target systems, aimed at bringing about defeat of the enemy as expeditiously as possible rather than allowing it to languish in relative safety while UN forces exhausted their resources by attacking supply routes that were not as important in a static war.

The new direction for the use of air power began with hydroelectric plants. Hitting those targets was meant not only to deter North Korea from pursuing the war, but also China, as some of the border facilities supplied power to China as well. Next, the UN increased air pressure in an all-out assault on Pyongyang, which the JCS cleared for attack in early July. Operation Pressure Pump on 11 July involved 1254 sorties from Fifth Air Force, US Navy, US Marine Corps, Republic of Korean, Australian, South African and British aircraft by day, and 54 SHORAN-directed B-29s at night.

The UN air campaign did not actually force the enemy to armistice talks, but it did have a profound psychological effect on the enemy. It was most successful in punishing Chinese

PSYWAR (PSYCHOLOGICAL WARFARE)

PSYWAR LEAFLETS WARNING CIVILIANS to leave Pyongyang were dropped before the Operation Pressure Pump strike. The raid was designed to demonstrate the omnipotence of UN air power and to disrupt industrial activity in the city. Radio Pyongyang was knocked off the air for two days, but with power restored, announcers stated that the 'brutal' attacks had destroyed 1500 buildings and inflicted thousands of civilian casualties.

Pyongyang was not the only North Korean city or town attacked during the air pressure campaign. In the latter half of 1952, more than 30 joint maximum-effort air strikes were carried out against key industrial objectives. Targets included supply, power, manufacturing, mining, oil, and rail centres.

On 20 July, Fifth Air Force B-26s began using incendiary and demolition bombs in night attacks on enemy communications centres to destroy supply concentration points, vehicle repair areas and military installations in towns where damaged buildings were being utilized. Psywar activities continued to precede bombings on towns to warn civilians that attack was imminent. This style of psywar was argued against by the US State Department, whose job it was to handle all humanitarian issues and the concerns of other nations.

Psywar efforts waned in late 1952, but the bombing of North Korean towns and cities continued unabated. By early 1953, Far East Bomber Command considered small cities and towns the last vulnerable link in the supply and distribution system for the communist armies. By the middle of 1953, 40–90 per cent of North Korean towns had been destroyed by UN bombing.

armies and North Korean towns throughout the course of the war. Eighteen of 22 major cities were at least half obliterated by bombs, and most villages were reduced to a low, wide mound of violet ashes. That experience for North Koreans still remains ingrained in their memory of UN airpower, and North Korean programs to develop missiles and weapons of mass destruction have been motivated to a large extent by the desire to deter any future applications of air pressure.

AIR FORCES INVOLVED
Hitherto, the main focus of this chapter has been the air forces of the US military. While they formed the majority of the air forces that engaged in activity over the Korean Peninsula during the war, they were not the only forces. As part of the UN coalition, Australia, Canada, Greece, South Africa and Thailand contributed air units. Australia and Canada were the only members of the British Commonwealth forces to supply air units. The Royal Air Force (Britain) had a wing of Short Sunderland flying boats based at Iwakuni in Japan, but they did not participate in the major air campaigns over Korea.

Australia's 77th Fighter Squadron was the first foreign unit to arrive in Korea on 2 July 1950. It was attached to the 35th US Fighter Group. The 77th was personally requested by MacArthur because it flew Mustangs. The Mustang was considered the

Above: A railroad marshalling yard in North Korea is hit by a salvo of bombs dropped by B-26 'Invader' light bombers of the US Fifth Air Force as part of a strategy to destroy supply points for communist forces.

F-86 SABRE

Above: This F-86E was flown in Korea by Major William T. Whisner, who served with the 25th Fighter Interceptor Squadron, 51st Fighter Interceptor Wing. The F-86E was one of the new jet-propelled fighters that provided UN forces with air superiority during the Korean War.

The F-86 was the United States' first swept-wing fighter that could counter the swept-wing Soviet MiG-15 in high-speed dogfights in the Korean War. Considered one of the best and most important fighter aircraft in that war, the Sabre fought some of the earliest jet-to-jet battles in history. Such was its quality that it remained in front-line service into the early 1980s with some operators. It was the F-86A model that first went to war in Korea, where its primary opponent was the Soviet-built MiG-15. By the end of hostilities, F-86 pilots had shot down 792 MiGs, according to USAF records, achieving a kill ratio of about 8:1.

In order to provide a welcome increase in range, the Korean Sabres often carried underwing drop tanks. The additional fuel allowed the fighters to extend their duration in the 'MiG Alley' combat zone, but they were always in short supply. A production line was set up in Japan in an effort to increase provision of the tanks.

best long-range ground-attack aircraft in the theatre, and Gen. Stratemeyer considered the 77th the best Mustang outfit in Japan at the outset of the war.

Unfortunately, the 77th's endeavours in Korea have been masked by a tragic early event. A friendly fire incident occurred on 3 July 1950, when the squadron attacked a train full of US and South Korean troops on the main highway between Suwon and Pyongtaek, inflicting many casualties, 29 of them fatal. To the 77th's credit, it had originally questioned its operations in the area, believing that North Korean forces could not have been so far south, but was assured by Fifth Air Force controllers that the target was correct. Unfortunately, the press gave them a hard time, despite being cleared of responsibility.

The 77th did not encounter any air battles in the opening phase of the war. The only resistance it met was from enemy ground fire. For the two months following their arrival, the 77th, equipped with bombs, rockets and napalm, supported UN troops retreating before the North Korean advance. The squadron flew its first missions supporting the Australian Army on 5 November, when it attacked Chinese troops opposing the 3rd Battalion, Royal Australian Regiment, at Pakchon.

When the Mustangs that the 77th operated met with the enemy MiGs, the squadron realized they had become obsolete. It continued to fly Mustangs until April 1951, when it returned to Japan to retire the Mustangs and move to the jet-powered British Gloster Meteor. Initially, there were high hopes for the Meteor, but early losses against the MiG cast a shadow over the Australian unit once more, threatening its prestige. It was relegated to escort duty and local defence until December 1951, when it was allowed to assume offensive operations in the period when the air pressure strategy was in effect.

The Royal Canadian Air Force (RCAF) was also involved as part of the Commonwealth forces sent to Korea. The RCAF was not involved with a combat role since no jet fighter squadrons capable of the type of combat required in Korea were yet in service, and capable fighter squadrons that later did become operational were allocated to NATO duty in Europe.

Twenty-two RCAF fighter pilots, however, flew the North American F-86 Sabre on exchange duty with the United States Air Force (USAF) in Korea so that they could gain combat experience. The main contingent provided by the RCAF was the No. 426 Transport Squadron, which was involved with the transportation of personnel and supplies. During the war, 600 trans-Pacific flights were flown carrying 3000 tons of cargo and 13,000 passengers. The RCAF suffered no losses.

In November 1950, the South African 2nd Air Squadron joined the war and was attached to the US 18th Fighter Group. Known as the Flying Cheetahs, its primary responsibilities

Below: Royal Canadian Air Force personnel making plans before a mission. Canadian Army personnel flew with the USAF as forward air controllers in the 6147 Tactical Air Control Group, informally known as the 'Mosquitos'.

were close air support. Initially, it flew Mustangs until February 1953, when it was equipped with the F-86 Sabre. Since its main contribution was close air support and attacks on ground forces, the squadron's Mustangs were susceptible to ground fire. The Mustang was considered an excellent aircraft for its range, but its cooling system made it particularly vulnerable to ground fire. The jet-powered F-86 Sabre was far more effective against enemy ground forces. They remained in Korea until December 1953.

Greece and Thailand also contributed air units to the war effort in Korea. The Hellenic Air Force sent seven Douglas C-47 Dakota transport aircraft from the 13th Transport Aircraft Squadron to South Korea to assist the United Nations. Greek aircraft operated in Korea until May 1955, flying thousands of missions including air evacuations, personnel transport, intelligence gathering and supply flights. The Royal Thai Air Force supplied three Douglas C-47 Skytrain aircraft for transport duties in the Korean War.

While the UN coalition clearly won the air war, North Korean forces put up a good fight with their MiG fighters. The twin-engine MiG-15 jet fighter was developed for the Soviet Union in the late 1940s. In Korea, it outclassed straight-winged jet day fighters, which were largely relegated to ground-attack roles, and was quickly countered by the similar American swept-wing North American F-86 Sabre. The MiG-15 is often mentioned, along with the F-86 Sabre, as the best fighter aircraft of the Korean War. It is

Below: F-86 Sabres with the 51st Fighter Interceptor Wing, known as the Checkertails, prepare for combat at Suwon Air Base, 1952.

ROYAL CANADIAN AIR FORCE

This unit was part of the Commonwealth forces sent to Korea. The RCAF did not have a combat role, since no jet fighter squadrons capable of the type of combat required in Korea were yet in service, and capable fighter squadrons that later did become operational were allocated to NATO duty in Europe. Twenty-two RCAF fighter pilots, however, flew the North American F-86 Sabre on exchange duty with the United States Air Force (USAF) in Korea so that they could gain combat experience.

The main contingent provided by the RCAF was the No. 426 Transport Squadron, who was involved with the transportation of personnel and supplies in support of the war.

mentioned as such, because the F-86 Sabre jets were designed as a direct response to the MiG-15, which was causing havoc in the Korean skies against the outdated aircraft being used by the UN.

While technically a part of the Korean People's Air Force, the MiGs flown during the war were done so by World War II veteran Soviet pilots. They would fly the flag of China or North Korea, but it was Soviet air power that waged war in the air against the UN forces. Stalin, however, went to great lengths to keep Soviet involvement a secret, as even he was not yet willing to directly engage the UN. Flying under the flag of China or North Korea was the first step in his efforts at misdirection. The second provision was that, while in the air, Soviet pilots would communicate only in Mandarin or Korean; the use of Russian was banned. And finally, Russian pilots would under no circumstances approach the 38th Parallel or the coastline. This was to prevent their capture by the Americans.

MIG ALLEY
While ultimate success in the air war over Korea rested with the UN, the Soviet forces can claim one great feat. The most famous air battle of the war has been dubbed Black Tuesday, and this occurred in MiG Alley. MiG Alley was the name given by United

MIG-15

Technically a part of the Korean People's Air Force, MiG-15s were flown during the war by WWII veteran Soviet pilots. They would fly the flag of China or North Korea, but it was Soviet air power that waged war in the air against the UN forces.

The Mikoyan-Gurevich MiG-15 was developed to intercept bombers, but proved a highly effective dogfighter. It was widely exported, with examples serving in the Chinese air force as well as the forces of Warsaw Pact nations.

The Western powers became aware of the MiG-15 during the Korean War, when six MiGs clashed with a force of piston-engined P-51 Mustangs. Although the MiG-15 performed well, an upgraded version designated MiG-15bis was quickly put into service. This variant had a more powerful engine and lighter weight, improving range and performance.

MiGs flew out of Chinese bases, and could only be engaged once they crossed the Yalu River into Korea. Their presence changed the nature of the air war in Korea; up to that time the UN forces had air superiority and could operate against ground targets more or less at will. Losses of B-29 bombers mounted, forcing the move to less effective night missions, and air-to-air clashes became deadly for UN pilots.

This aircraft (illustrated) fought during the Korean War for the People's Liberation Army (PLA) in 1950. Note the prominent wing fences, which reduce the tendency of swept-wing aircraft to stall due to spanwise (rather than front-to-back) airflow over the wings.

Nations pilots to the northwestern portion of North Korea, where the Yalu River emptied into the Yellow Sea. It was the site of numerous dogfights between UN fighter pilots and their opponents from North Korea and the People's Republic of China.

On 23 October 1951, the Western air forces cobbled together an armada of 200 jet fighters (F-86 Sabres, F-84s, F-80s and British-built Gloster Meteor IVs) and nearly two dozen

B-29 Superfortress bombers. Their mission was to provide a concentrated attack to disrupt the flow of supplies to Korean and Chinese forces and to put the airbases at Naamsi and Taechon in North Korea out of action. They were countered by two fighter air divisions. The 303rd, comprising 58 MiG-15s, formed the first echelon and was assigned to attack the primary group of enemy bombers and fighter-bombers. The 324th division had 26 MiG-15s and comprised the second echelon.

The Russian strategy was to ignore the fighter escorts and go straight for the slower Superfortresses. The MiGs tore into the B-29 formations. Some of the Russian pilots attacked the American bombers vertically from below, seeing the B-29s explode in front of their eyes. It was almost a turkey shoot, as the crew of the stricken bombers bailed out one by one. The Russians claimed the destruction of ten B-29s – the highest percentage of US bombers ever lost on a major mission – and lost only one MiG.

Black Tuesday would forever change the USAF's conduct of strategic aerial bombardment. The B-29s would no longer fly daytime sorties into MiG Alley. North Korean towns and villages would no longer be carpet-bombed and napalmed by the Americans. Thousands of civilians were out of the firing line. More important to the overall war effort, however, was the fact that Russian suppression of the B-29s might have prevented the dropping of nuclear bombs and the escalation of the Korean War on the world stage.

Above: USAF pilots walk through the famous *torii* gate leading to the Sabre flight line at Kimpo Airfield. There, they flew to the northwestern portion of North Korea known as 'MiG Alley' – a region known for the most harrowing dogfights between the US F-86 Sabre and the Soviet MiG-15.

ATOMIC AND CONVENTIONAL BOMBING

The United States considered using atomic weapons several times during the Korean War. The closest it came to doing so was in April 1951, when MacArthur was being relieved of command.

On 10 March 1951, MacArthur had requested permission to use atomic weapons to maintain air superiority in the Korean theatre, after intelligence reports suggested that Soviet forces appeared ready to move air divisions to the vicinity of Korea and put Soviet bombers into air bases in Manchuria, from which they could strike not just Korea, but American bases in Japan.

On 15 April, the JCS ordered immediate atomic retaliation against Manchurian bases if large numbers of troops came into the fighting, or if it appeared that bombers were being launched against American assets from there.

The threat was real, as atomic cores were transferred to the Far East Command. In this instance, nuclear technology was not pursued, and President Truman used MacArthur's posture against him in the ensuing battle between the two magnates. The JCS entertained the idea of using nuclear technology again in June 1951 in a tactical application. Project Vista was actually devised to determine the feasibility of using tactical atomic weapons, but the potential for damage to civilian populations eventually negated any further talk of the use of atomic bombs.

While the atomic bomb was never deployed in the Korean War, an unrelenting bombing campaign upon the enemy ensued that created irrevocable damage. When Gen. Dean, the commander of the 25th Infantry, was released after spending the war in captivity, he was amazed at the destruction of the Korean landscape. The city of Huichon, he noted, had been filled with two-storied buildings and a prominent main street

Below: July 1951. The remnants of US bombing missions at Sinuiju, a North Korean town that sits along the Yalu River.

at the outset of the war. When he was released, none of that remained. The villages were in rubble and nothing else was left. Others recounted that there was nothing left between the Yalu River and Pyongyang. North Korean cities simply no longer existed. According the US Airforce estimates, the scale of urban destruction in North Korea exceeded the damage inflicted upon Germany and Japan during World War II.

HUMAN TOLL

In 1984, Curtis Lemay, the head of the Strategic Air Command, the organizer of bombings over Japan and Korea, noted that the bombing of North Korea had killed 20 per cent of the population. Other sources cite a somewhat lower number. According to a data set developed by researchers at the Centre for the Study of Civil War (CSCW) and the International Peace Research Institute, Oslo (PRIO), the 'best estimate' of civilian deaths in North Korea is 995,000, with a low estimate of 645,000 and a high estimate of 1.5 million.

> THE 'BEST ESTIMATE' OF CIVILIAN DEATHS IN NORTH KOREA IS 995,000.

Interestingly, the CSCW/PRIO estimate of 995,000 deaths still exceeds the civilian death tolls of any other bombing campaign, including the Allied firebombing of German cities in World War II, which claimed an estimated 400,000–600,000 lives; the firebombing and nuclear bombing of Japanese cities, which caused an estimated 330,000–900,000 deaths; and the bombing of Indochina from 1964 to 1973, which caused an estimated 121,000–361,000 deaths overall.

More important, however, is the Korean death toll in comparison with the relatively modest population of the country: just 9.7 million people in 1950. By comparison, there were 65 million people in Germany and 72 million people in Japan at the end of World War II. The attacks by the US Air Force against North Korea used the firebombing tactics that had been developed in the World War II bombing of Europe and Japan: explosives to break up buildings, napalm and other incendiaries to ignite massive fires, and strafing to prevent fire-fighting crews from extinguishing the blazes. But public opinion at the close of World War II and the US policy of not attacking civilians curtailed the bombing campaigns at the outset of the war. When the Chinese entered the war en masse, however, MacArthur broke with previous policy and issued a statement to Gen. Stratemeyer to burn and destroy as a lesson to any of those towns that he considered of military value to the enemy.

Stratemeyer interpreted MacArthur's commands to mean that every installation, facility and village in North Korea was a military and tactical target. Stratemeyer sent orders to the Fifth Air Force and Bomber Command to 'destroy every means of communications and every installation, factory, city, and village.' In May 1951, an international fact-finding team sent to assess the damage of the UN air war did not see one town that had not been destroyed, and there were very few undamaged villages.

UN bombings were made exponentially worse by the severity of North Korean winters. Temperatures reached 40°C below freezing (-40°F) during the winter. Since the most severe bombing took place in November 1950, those who escaped immediate death by fire were left at risk of death by exposure in the days and months that followed. Survivors created makeshift shelters in canyons, caves or abandoned cellars. Those left without supplies succumbed to the harshness of the winter.

In May 1951, a visiting delegation to the bombed city of Sinuiju from the Women's International Democratic Federation (WIDF) reported that the overwhelming majority of the inhabitants lived in dugouts made of earth supported from salvaged timber. Others were living in cellars that remained after the bombardment and still others in thatched tents within the framework of destroyed buildings and in huts made of unmortared brick and rubble.

The ground war in Korea during the first phase of the conflict was characterized by North Korean and UN forces going back and forth until political concerns led to a stalemate. That was not the case in the air war. The UN command released an unrelenting

NAPALM

WHILE THE THREAT FROM the severe winters was a problem, it was not the only one associated with the fallout of the UN bombing campaign. The extensive use of napalm also wreaked havoc upon the North Korean population. The sticky, flammable substance was first used in World War II but became a key weapon during the Korean War, where 29,535 tonnes (32,557 tons) of it were deployed against the enemy.

Napalm was originally developed in 1942 in a secret laboratory at Harvard University by a team led by chemist Louis Fieser under the United States Chemical Warfare Service. Initially developed for use as an incendiary service in World War II, it was soon viewed as a valuable commodity in Korea for close air support. It remained useful in that capacity throughout the Korean War, and later in Vietnam, because of its effectiveness against dug-in enemy personnel. The burning incendiary composition flowed into foxholes, trenches

Above: US Air Force B-26 'Invaders' drop napalm on a railroad junction at Munchon, North Korea.

and bunkers, and drainage and irrigation ditches and other improvised troop shelters. Napalm meant that North Koreans had no chance of escape.

campaign against North Korea. They quickly gained control of the skies, which translated into their ability to launch unopposed naval and air interdictions against North Korean forces. In the end, they destroyed the North Korean landscape and left nothing in its wake. The ferocity of the UN air campaign fuelled North Korean directives long after the armistice, and provided a constant reminder of the need to develop counter-measures against the air capabilities of the UN and, more importantly, the US.

5

STALEMATE

For all practical purposes, the Korean War ended on 30 June 1951, after UN Supreme Commander Matthew Ridgway signalled his willingness to discuss truce terms with the communist forces. The original North Korean attack and the subsequent Chinese entry had been contained.

THE UNITED STATES, and therefore the UN, had nothing left to gain from continued fighting. The goal of saving South Korea had been accomplished. North Korea could also claim a semblance of victory. While they ended up with no territorial gain, they had fought the power of the US and UN to a standstill and demonstrated to the world that Asian races were not inferior to Western powers – a myth that had been exacerbated by Japan's defeat in World War II.

During the Kaesong talks on 30 July, all parties agreed that hostilities should continue even while negotiations were in progress. That decision led to political turmoil in the United States, as the Truman Administration had to defend why it was still keeping soldiers in Korea despite both sides wishing to pursue peace. The stalemate war seemed a needless waste of American lives that the citizenry could not cope with.

The generals in the field also found the situation tough. It was not in their nature or training to sit idly by. While peace negations ensued, they were ordered to fight on, but not too

Opposite: A US Marine from the 1st Marine Division uses a flamethrower to burn out positions which could conceal North Korean snipers, a common practice in the hill fights during the stalemate phase of the war.

hard: don't lose, but don't win. With their hands tied behind their backs, they were to wage a truly limited war while the diplomats worked on negotiations.

If commanders felt hampered by their situation, the men on the front were more bewildered by their predicament. They knew that any order they were given would be limited, and that their actions would not have any real effect on the war. It was not the same as it had been in the first year of the war, when there were clear objectives. As such, morale quickly declined. The men constantly looked for word from Kaesong, hoping that the war would be over and they could return home.

On 1 July, roughly 750,000 Chinese and North Korean troops stood across the line from half a million UN troops. Eighth Army commanders had been preparing offensives when the talks at Kaesong began, the objectives of which were to capture hills such as the Punchbowl or Fool's Mountain, or to deny ground to the enemy. The North Koreans, however, had dug in, much like the Japanese had in World War II. They had gone underground into elaborate tunnel systems in the sides of the mountains.

Below: 13 August 1951: UN delegates attend peace talks at Kaesong during the Korean War. From left to right: Major-General Henry I. Hodes; Major-General L.C. Craigie (USAF); Vice-Admiral Turner Joy (USN), the chief UN delegate; Major-General Paik Sun Yup of the Republic of Korea Army; and Rear Admiral Arleigh A. Burke.

Above: Medical staff at the 121st Evacuation Hospital at Yongdong-pu gather around a seriously wounded soldier of the 116th Engineers, prior to operating.

BLOODY RIDGE

The Battle of Bloody Ridge began as an attempt by UN forces to seize a ridge of hills that they believed were being used as observation posts to call in artillery fire on a UN supply road. It consisted of three hills – 983, 940 and 773 – and their connecting ridges. Four razor-back ridges converged on the western extremity of Bloody Ridge to form Hill 983, a sharp and well-defined point and the highest peak of the ridgeline. To the east, separated from 983 by a steep draw, the 1000m-long (3280ft) centre section of Bloody Ridge came to a peak at Hill 940. Another 900m (3000ft) east of this peak was Hill 773. US X Corps commander Maj. Gen. Clovis E. Byers was ordered to eliminate important observation posts of the Korean People's Army (KPA) that directed heavy and accurate artillery fire upon the Line Kansas position from the ridge, some 3km (2 miles) west and slightly south of Hill 1179. The US 2nd Infantry Division, augmented by the ROK 36th Regiment, 5th Infantry Division, were ordered to take this east–west ridge, which they later named Bloody Ridge due to the intense fighting that occurred there.

The maze of enemy trenches on the ridges made it appear to air observers that Bloody Ridge had been ploughed. The trenches connected many bunkers that the enemy had built strong enough to withstand artillery fire and air strikes. The larger ones sheltered as many as 60 men. Some protected small artillery pieces or mortars. Detection of enemy positions from the ground was difficult because the hills were partially wooded and enemy soldiers had been skilful with camouflage.

The battle began on 17 August 1951. The ROK 36th Regiment assaulted the ridge, but had to withdraw under heavy KPA pressure to the tune of over a thousand casualties. Continuing to press forward, the ROK 36th finally took the hill on 25 August. Victory was short-lived, however. The following day, they were forced off the hill by the enemy. On 27 August, the 9th Infantry, which had placed its 2nd Battalion in supporting positions on Hill 940, attempted to seize Hill 983, without success.

Above: A US Marine catching up on much needed sleep after intense hill fights on the central front.

The 2nd Battalion withdrew that evening, going all the way back to Worun-ni. The following day, the 3rd Battalion, attacking the long ridge from the east, failed to reach even the first objective. Faced with a surprise attack that night, it also fell back to Worun-ni. Thus, before the 1st Battalion made its first attack against the Bloody Ridge hill mass, UN forces had captured the long ridgeline only to lose it again, hill by hill.

On 30 August, the 9th Infantry made a frontal assault, sending its 1st and 2nd Battalions straight north against Hill 940. Both battalions got within a few hundred yards of the top of the ridgeline before enemy fire halted the advance. When it became apparent that neither battalion would reach the objective before dark, the regimental commander ordered both to withdraw.

The withdrawal took until 4.00 a.m. on 31 August. The entire 1st Battalion reassembled in the area it had occupied before the attack. There was talk of an imminent enemy attack. Tired and hungry, the men were denied their much-needed rest after fleeing their forward positions, as they had to remain alert. While they received rations, sleep still proved an elusive concept. After waiting a few hours with no attack, the battalion was moved by trucks to an assembly area south of Worun-ni, where the companies reorganized before another planned attack on another hill.

At noon on 31 August, some eight hours after having fled from the enemy on Hill 940, the 1st Battalion was loaded on trucks again and rode 3km (2 miles) forward, where it was tasked with taking Hill 773, this time from the east. At the eastern tip of the ridgeline, where Bloody Ridge ended at the road pass between Worun-ni and the Pia-ri Valley, Company C turned left and climbed towards the first knoll on the ridgeline leading towards Hill 773. The knoll was already in friendly hands, but morning fog obscured the way forward. The peaks of hills 773 and 940 were completely covered by the haze, making the forward path invisible beyond the first observation point. An enemy machine gun suddenly commenced firing from a knoll 90–180m (295–590ft) beyond the front of the column, setting off a ten-minute firefight. The fog had an equal effect on the enemy, who could not aim correctly without clear visibility. With the supporting fire of four

Below: American soldiers securing the top of the hill known as 'Bloody Ridge', the first in a series of hills believed to be used as observation posts to call in artillery fire on a UN supply road.

machine guns, the Americans advanced without incident and against negligible enemy fire.

While the fog was initially a blessing, elements of the 2nd Division soon realized that the enemy had only stopped firing because they, too, could not see through it to assess the opposing force. On 1 September the fog cleared, and the enemy fire began once again. The 2nd Division continued to press forward against a well-dug-in enemy. For the next few days, UN forces used air attacks, flamethrowers and grenades to bust up the tunnels that permeated the hills in front of them. On 3 September, Hills 940 and 983 were taken without opposition. The enemy had apparently moved north to strengthen positions on the next prominent terrain feature in that area: Heartbreak Ridge. Heartbreak Ridge would be an even greater test to the resolve of both sides of the conflict.

THE PUNCHBOWL

In late August, three regiments of the US 1st Marine Division were given orders to move from their reserve areas around Inje County to support the UN offensive. One of their main responsibilities was to distract People's Volunteer Army (PVA) and KPA reinforcements from the Battle of Bloody Ridge. Bloody Ridge had turned into a bitter give-and-take struggle between the 2nd Division and dug-in KPA forces. The 1st Marine Division was ordered to attack Yoke Ridge and advance to a new defensive line to be called the Hays Line, marked by the southern edge of the Soyang River to the north of the Punchbowl. On 30 August, in preparation for the attack, a battalion of 1st Korean Marine Corps Regiment (1st KMC) occupied Hill 793 on the eastern edge of the Punchbowl between the Kansas Line and Yoke Ridge.

Above: US Marines launch a 4.5-inch (114-mm) rocket barrage against Chinese forces. Such attacks were frequent occurrences during the 'Outpost War', where rockets would be fired from trenches on enemy hill positions.

At 6.00 a.m. on 31 August, the 7th Marine Regiment and two battalions of the 1st KMC launched the assault with an attack from Hill 793 up the eastern edge of the Punchbowl towards Yoke Ridge in the west and Tonpyong in the east. By late morning, the assault units had reached Yoke Ridge and were engaging the KPA defenders. By the end of the first day, the UN force occupied the southeastern end of Yoke Ridge.

On 1 September, the 1st KMC moved west along Yoke Ridge, while the 7th Marines moved north, clearing out KPA bunkers with grenades and flamethrowers. The KPA launched several small-scale counter-attacks against the advancing Marines, but these were broken up by small-arms and mortar fire, artillery and several airstrikes. The UN forces consolidated their positions in the evening under KPA mortar and artillery fire. That night, the KPA launched an attack under the cover of darkness on the 1st KMC on Hill 924, driving them out of the position they had secured earlier that day.

On the morning of 2 September, supported by heavy artillery fire, the 1st KMC recaptured Hill 924 and moved further west towards its next objective, Hill 1026. After beating back several small KPA attacks, 3rd Battalion 7th Marines had siezed Hill 602 by early afternoon. The KPA launched several company-size counter-attacks on Hill 602, all of which were beaten back. In many ways, the nature of the battle transpiring near the Punchbowl mirrored the give-and-take nature of the battle that was still raging on Bloody Ridge.

In the afternoon of 3 September, the 1st KMC renewed their attack on Hill 1026, while 2nd Battalion, 7th Marines assumed the defence of Hill 924. As they advanced, the 1st KMC encountered a large KPA force advancing towards Hill 924. The 1st KMC forced back the KPA and seized Hill 1026 by midday, beating back a KPA counter-attack and advancing northwest to seize Hill 1055 and west to take Hill 930, thus securing all of Yoke Ridge. Meanwhile, to the west of the Punchbowl, ROK 35th Regiment, 5th Division advanced unopposed from the Kansas Line to Hill 450, approximately 3.3km (2 miles)

Below: An American Sherman tank advances towards a North Korean roadblock as infantrymen look for concealed enemies, September 1951.

southwest of Hill 1026, while the US 2nd Infantry Division took Hill 1181, 4km (2.5 miles) southwest of Hill 930. Once Yoke Bridge was secure, phase two of the campaign began.

SECOND PHASE

The second phase of the campaign occurred between 4 and 10 September at Kanmubong Ridge. It was considered essential to seize Kanmubong Ridge, immediately north of Yoke Ridge, in order to defend the Hays Line and to allow US X Corps to attack the KPA's main line of resistance, which was believed to be located approximately 3km (2 miles) north of it. The 1st Marine Division and 1st KMC consolidated their positions on Yoke Ridge, established the Hays Line, and built up ammunition and supplies for the attack on Kanmubong Ridge. The KPA used the lull in fighting to reinforce their positions on Hill 673, opposite Hill 602. Both sides actively patrolled the area.

The 7th Marines received orders to launch an attack at 3.00 a.m. on 11 September from the Hays Line through a narrow valley, across a tributary of the Soyang River and then uphill towards Hills 680 and 673, with Hill 749 as a further objective. Supporting the 7th Marines would be the 1st Tank Battalion, with artillery support from the 11th Marine Regiment. The 3rd Battalion, 7th Marines were tasked with capturing Hill 680. Despite extensive artillery fire to prepare for their attack, progress was slow, with the KPA defenders able to provide interlocking fire from their bunkers. By the end of the day, 3rd Battalion, 7th Marines were forced to dig in 90m (300ft) south of the summit. The 1st Battalion, 7th Marines were tasked with capturing Hill 673, but strong opposition from the KPA bunkers forced them to stop short of their objective.

> WHEN NIGHT FELL ON 11 SEPTEMBER, 2ND BATTALION, 7TH MARINES MOVED TO THE REAR OF HILL 673, CUTTING OFF THE KPA TROOPS THERE.

When night fell on 11 September, 2nd Battalion, 7th Marines moved to the rear of Hill 673, cutting off the KPA troops there. By 2pm the next day, Hill 673 had been secured. That night, 12 September, the 1st Marine Regiment relieved 1st and 3rd

Battalions, 7th Marines on Hill 673; 2nd Battalion, 7th Marines could not be relieved, as they were closely engaged on Hill 749, but 2nd Battalion, 1st Marines moved forward to relieve them the following day.

On 13 September, 2nd Battalion, 1st Marines were ordered to seize Hill 749 and then move northwest to take Hills 812, 980 and 1052, while 3rd Battalion, 1st Marines would move west from Hill 680 to take Hill 751 and then attack northwest to Hill 1052. Hill 749 proved to be a heavily defended fortress of bunkers, covered trenches and tunnels and part of the KPA main line of resistance. 2nd Battalion, 1st Marines seized the summit at midday, but were soon driven back.

They finally gained control of the summit three hours later, but it would be nearly 8.00 p.m. before they could relieve 2nd

Below: Members of the 1st Marine Division take respite near a Korean hut after destroying an enemy sniper housed there, September 1951.

THIRD GENEVA CONVENTION

ON 12 AUGUST 1949, the Third Geneva Convention convened to replace the Prisoners of War Convention of 1929. Prisoner of war status and laws governing treatment while in captivity were more clearly defined. More important for the Korean War, the Convention established the principle that prisoners of war should be released and repatriated without delay after the cessation of active hostilities. This was the major issue that negotiators fought over in peace talks at Kaesong and Panmunjom.

Battalion, 7th Marines on the reverse slope of the hill. The 3rd Battalion, 1st Marines' advance towards Hill 751 was delayed by mines and the more urgent need for supporting arms on Hill 749. By evening, they dug in short of Hill 751, where they endured mortar fire and 10 KPA counter-attacks during the night. September saw the first operational use of Marine helicopters in combat, with the HRS-1 helicopters of HMR-161, operating from forward base X-83 near Cheondo-ri, conducting 28 flights to resupply the Marines near Hill 793 and evacuate 74 casualties.

The battle continued in this manner for the next several days. The Marines would take a hill only to relinquish it the following day. The battle for a better main line position appeared to drag on with no end in sight. After midnight on 20 September, the KPA launched an intense mortar and artillery barrage on the Marines between The Rock and Hill 812. On the same day, east of the Kanmubong Range, the ROK 8th Infantry Division struggled to secure Hill 854. The 1st Marines were ordered to assist the 8th ROK, but the attack did not begin until evening and the forces quickly became bogged down against stiff resistance. On 21 September, 3rd Battalion, 1st Marines resumed the assault on Hill 854; by 17:45, it had been secured.

HEARTBREAK RIDGE
In the west, a second great battle for command of the hills was already under way. After UN forces withdrew from Bloody

Opposite: Heartbreak Ridge (seen here from the north) followed the hill fight on Bloody Ridge. Between 13 September and 15 October 1951, bitter struggles for control of the ridge often descended into hand-to-hand fighting.

> THE INEVITABLE COUNTER-ATTACK SOON CAME — WAVES OF NORTH KOREANS DETERMINED TO RECAPTURE THE LOST GROUND AT ANY COST.

Ridge, the North Koreans set up new positions just 1400m (4500ft) away on an 11km-long (7 mile) hill mass. That hill was soon dubbed 'Heartbreak Ridge' due to the bitter struggle that took place for control of it from 13 September to 15 October 1951. Communist defences were even more formidable there than on Bloody Ridge.

US 2nd Infantry Division's acting commander, Brig. Gen. Thomas Deshazo, and his immediate superior, Maj. Gen. Byers, the X Corps commander, seriously underestimated the strength of the North Korean position. They ordered a single infantry regiment, the 23rd, and its attached French Battalion, to make an ill-conceived assault straight up Heartbreak's heavily fortified slopes. All three of the 2nd Division's infantry regiments participated, with the brunt of the combat borne by the 9th and 23rd Infantry Regiments, along with the attached French Battalion. The initial attack began on 13 September and quickly deteriorated into a familiar pattern.

First, American aircraft, tanks and artillery would pummel the ridge for hours on end, turning the already barren hillside into a cratered moonscape. Next, the 23rd's infantrymen would clamber up the mountain's rocky slopes, taking out one enemy bunker after another by direct assault. Those who survived to reach the crest arrived exhausted and low on ammunition. The inevitable counter-attack soon came – waves of North Koreans determined to recapture the lost ground at any cost. Many of these counter-attacks were conducted at night by fresh troops that the North Koreans were able to bring up under the shelter of neighbouring hills. Battles begun by a bomb, bullet and shell were inevitably finished by grenade, trench knife and fists as formal military engagements degenerated into desperate hand-to-hand brawls. Sometimes, dawn broke to reveal the defenders still holding the mountaintop.

The battle progressed for two weeks. Because of the constricting terrain and the narrow confines of the objectives, units were committed piecemeal, one platoon, company or

battalion at a time. Once a unit could no longer stand the strain, a replacement would take its place until the 23rd Infantry as a whole was almost shattered. Several units were wiped out.

The Americans employed massive artillery barrages, airstrikes and tanks in attempts to drive the North Koreans off the ridge, but the KPA proved extremely hard to dislodge. Finally, on 27 September, the 2nd Division's new commander, Maj. Gen. Robert N. Young, called a halt to the attacks on Heartbreak Ridge as American planners reconsidered their strategy. As long as the North Koreans could continue to reinforce and resupply their garrison on the ridge, it would be nearly impossible for the Americans to take the mountain.

When American leaders had their 'light-bulb' moment – when they realized another strategy was needed – they devised a new plan that called for a full division-sized assault on the valleys and hills adjacent to Heartbreak to cut the ridge off from further reinforcement. Spearheading this offensive would be the 72nd Tank Battalion, whose mission was to push up the Mundung-ni Valley west of Heartbreak to destroy enemy supply dumps.

It was a bold plan, but one that could not be accomplished until a way had been found to get the 72nd's Sherman tanks into the valley. The only existing road was little more than a track that could not bear the weight of the Shermans. To make matters worse, the road was mined and blocked by a 2m-high (6ft) rock barrier built by the North Koreans. Using shovels and explosives, the men of the 2nd Division's 2nd Engineer Combat Battalion braved enemy fire to clear these obstacles and build an improved roadway. While they worked, the division's three infantry

Below: The US 2nd Infantry Division, tasked with the main responsibility of securing Heartbreak Ridge, fire an 81mm (3.18in) mortar at the enemy.

SHERMAN M4A3

The M4 Sherman was by far the most numerous Allied tank of World War II. Almost 50,000 were built, with many variants and derivatives. Shermans remained in service many years after the war, with examples surviving into the 1990s. During the Korean War, the United States kept the M4A3 'Easy Eight' in service, usually armed with the powerful 76mm (3in) gun. The lighter M4A3(76) W HVSS tank (illustrated below) was appreciated for its mechanical reliability compared to the heavier M26 Pershing. The M4A3(76) Sherman and the Russian-supplied T-34/85 had similar abilities and could destroy each other at normal combat ranges – although better crew training and the use of advanced optics and High Velocity Armor Piercing ammunition gave the Sherman an advantage.

regiments – 9th, 23rd and 38th – launched coordinated assaults on Heartbreak Ridge and the adjacent hills.

By 10 October, everything was ready for the main operation. On 11 October, led by more than 30 tanks and supported by artillery and airplanes, the 2nd Division started advancing into the valley. The sudden onslaught of a battalion of tanks racing up the valley took the enemy by surprise. By coincidence, the thrust came just when the Chinese 204th Division was moving up to

relieve the North Koreans on Heartbreak Ridge. The Chinese unit under fire was the 610th Regiment of the 204th Division. The regiment's mission was to reinforce the North Korean defence along the valley against a possible American armoured offensive; more specifically, it was ordered to prevent the Americans from reaching the town of Mundung-ni at all costs.

Before the Chinese could dig in, the 2nd Division had already started the attack. Caught in the open, the Chinese division suffered heavy casualties from the American tanks as the armoured vehicles penetrated to a depth of 6km (4 miles) of the Chinese defence lines and caused great damage. However, the 610th Regiment managed to damage five Sherman tanks before the Americans halted the offensive.

On 12 October, the 2nd Division began an airborne and artillery bombardment that lasted for two hours on Hill 635 and Hill 709 before the 23rd Regiment, led by 48 tanks, assaulted Chinese defensive positions. Having learned the American tactics from the previous day, the 610th Regiment of the Chinese Army had already reinforced the anti-tank trenches flanking the road that ran through the Mundung-ni Valley. Chinese soldiers fired upon the advancing American tanks at point-blank range, damaging 18 of the American tanks.

The 23rd Regiment did not assault the hills on the next day. The South Korean 8th Division, however, starting from 13 October, launched its attack on hills 97, 742, 650, 932 and 922. These battles were as brutal and costly as those that preceded them, but the ROK Army took the hill on its eleventh assault on 14 October. Eight Shermans attacked the Chinese positions along Mundung-ni Valley. All the tanks were knocked out by the crossfire of Chinese anti-tank guns. Two more were lost on 19 October due to mines.

Over the five days, the Shermans roared up and down the Mundung-ni Valley, overrunning supply dumps, mauling troop concentrations and destroying approximately 350 bunkers on Heartbreak and in the surrounding hills and valleys. A smaller

Opposite: Infantrymen of the 27th Infantry Regiment, near Heartbreak Ridge, take advantage of cover and concealment in tunnel positions, 10 August 1952.

THESE BATTLES WERE AS BRUTAL ... AS THOSE THAT PRECEDED THEM, BUT THE ROK ARMY TOOK THE HILL ON ITS ELEVENTH ASSAULT ON 14 OCTOBER.

tank infantry team scoured the Sat'ae-ri Valley east of the ridge, thereby completing the encirclement and eliminating any hope of reinforcement for the beleaguered North Koreans on the ridge.

The armoured thrusts turned the tide of the battle, but plenty of hard fighting remained for the infantry before French soldiers captured the last communist bastion on the ridge on 13 October. After 30 days of combat, the Americans and French eventually gained the upper hand and secured Heartbreak Ridge. Yet the Sherman tanks did not penetrate through the Mundung-ni Valley and reach the town of Mundung-ni. The Defence of Mundung-ni is still celebrated by North Korea as a great victory, despite the heavy losses they incurred on Heartbreak Ridge.

RENEWED PEACE TALKS

On 25 October, UN and communist negotiators reconvened truce talks at a new location, a collection of tents in the tiny village of Panmunjom, 10km (6 miles) east of Kaesong. After some sparring, the communists dropped their demand for a return to the 38th Parallel and accepted the UN position that the ceasefire line be drawn along the current line of contact. In exchange, the UN bowed to communist demands that a truce line be agreed upon prior to the resolution of other outstanding issues.

> THE TERMINATION OF THE UN OFFENSIVE AND THE RESUMPTION OF TRUCE TALKS IN LATE OCTOBER HAD A NOTICEABLY CALMING EFFECT ON THE FRONT.

To avoid the danger that the communists might stop negotiating once a line had been established, the Americans insisted that both sides be permitted to continue fighting until all outstanding questions had been resolved. The two sides also agreed that the proposed armistice line would only be valid for 30 days. Should a final truce not be arrived at within that time, then the agreement over the line of demarcation would be invalid.

The willingness of the United Nations to accept the current line of contact as the final line of demarcation between the two Koreas represented a significant windfall for the communists: it served as a fairly strong indicator that the United Nations had no

Above: UN delegates meet with representatives of the communists to negotiate an armistice agreement at Panmunjom, Korea, 1 November 1951.

desire to press deeper into North Korea. The termination of the UN offensive and the resumption of truce talks in late October had a noticeably calming effect on the front.

On 12 November, Ridgway instructed Gen. Van Fleet to assume an 'active defense'. Van Fleet went one step further by prohibiting his subordinates from initiating any offensive operations other than counter-attacks to recapture ground lost to an enemy attack. Nobody wanted another Bloody Ridge or Heartbreak Ridge, and the US could not justify the losses to the American public in an increasingly less popular conflict. The communists likewise refrained from undertaking major actions, and the resulting lull gave the UN the opportunity to accomplish a major change in battlefield line-up.

Between December 1951 and February 1952, the United States withdrew the 1st Cavalry and 24th Infantry Divisions from Korea and replaced them with two National Guard formations, the 40th and 45th Infantry Divisions. While the Army realigned its order of battle, the Panmunjom negotiators struggled to finalize the truce. While the lack of a truce usually signalled a renewal of hostilities,

Above: 'Freedom Gate Bridge' spanning the Imjin River, built by the 84th Engineer Construction Battalion, 10 March 1952. This bridge temporarily replaced the original structure which was destroyed by bombs.

the harshness of the Korean winter served to prevent anything more than patrols and posturing by both sides. Commanders in the field on both sides seemed content to sit out the winter and let the negotiators do the heavy fighting. As had been the case on many prior occasions, the negotiators were all too willing to continue the fight, and a truce remained out of reach.

NEGOTIATIONS IN TROUBLE

Communist agents in the POW camps were ordered to begin disruptive activities. Armed with homemade weapons, pro-communist elements deftly employed intimidation and violence to gain control of the interiors of many POW camps. Then, in early May, communist prisoners scored a stunning coup when they succeeded in capturing Brig. Gen. Francis T. Dodd, the commandant of the UN's main POW camp on Koje-do. To achieve his release, American authorities pledged to suspend additional repatriation screenings in a poorly-worded communiqué that seemed to substantiate communist allegations that the UN had previously mistreated prisoners.

PRISONER EXCHANGE

A NUMBER OF ISSUES separated UN and communist negotiators during the winter of 1951–52. Chief among them was the exchange of prisoners. Both sides had pledged to abide by the Geneva Convention of 1949, which called for the immediate and complete exchange of all prisoners upon the conclusion of hostilities. This seemingly straightforward principle, however, disturbed many Americans. More than 40,000 South Korean captives that had been impressed into service by the NKPA and Chinese were detained in UN prisoner camps. There were many Chinese prisoners that were also impressed by the PVA – the Nationalists.

Many of those expressed no desire to return north, leaving the UN with a moral dilemma. How could they repatriate people who expressed a desire not to return to their home countries? Memories of repatriation after World War II, when Soviet detainees were released only to be mistreated, imprisoned or even killed by their own government, affected US President Truman, who was ultimately responsible for policy concerning prisoner exchange. Also important to him was the potential publicity he could gain against communists in the greater Cold War if he erred on the side of morality. The Chinese and North Koreans, however, were also well aware of the potential political outfall from their inability to return prisoners, so they chose to dig their heels in, only entertaining the idea of a complete exchange or nothing.

Left: Chinese and North Korean prisoners assembled at the United Nations' prisoner-of-war camp at Pusan, April 1951.

OPERATION COUNTER

OPERATION COUNTER IS ONE example of some of the larger outpost battles. This was an attempt by American forces to attack and occupy 12 Chinese outposts, including Hill 266 near Ch'orwon. The hill was very important, as it gave a strategic advantage to its possessor for miles in all directions. The 45th Infantry Division, tasked with the job of securing these outposts, easily seized 11 of its 12 objectives during a night assault on 6 June, with the twelfth falling into American hands six days later during a second-phase attack.

The Chinese did not give up, however. The 45th successively repulsed 20 Chinese attacks, but Chinese perseverance paid off when they managed to push elements of the 2nd Infantry Division off one of these outposts later in the month – a key mountain 14km (9 miles) west of Ch'orwon known as Old Baldy. Battles like Old Baldy occurred on countless mountain peaks and ridges during 1952, as the two sides struggled to gain control over the rugged terrain that separated their respective battle lines.

Above: Soldiers digging into bunkers atop Old Baldy. Old Baldy, Hill 266 near Ch'orwon, was the site of one of the larger outpost battles during Operation Counter in 1952.

The episode humiliated the United Nations Command (UNC) and handed communist negotiators and propagandists alike a new weapon that they wielded with great zeal, both within the negotiating tent and on the larger stage of world public opinion. As positions at the negotiating table hardened, a return to hostilities seemed imminent.

During the winter, the Chinese had fortified their positions and moved in a massive force. By the spring of 1952, 200,000 UN forces stood against an enemy of 900,000. By June, communist guns were hurling shells daily at UN positions, and the UN artillery responded in kind. Nor did a day go by when communist and UN soldiers did not clash somewhere along the frontline. One of the most common missions performed by UN infantrymen was the small raid for the purpose of capturing enemy prisoners for interrogation. These operations were usually launched at night and were extremely dangerous – indeed, relatively few succeeded in capturing any prisoners.

> AT THIS LEVEL, THE WAR WAS A VERY PERSONAL AFFAIR — IT WAS MAN AGAINST MAN, RIFLE AGAINST GRENADE, FIST AGAINST KNIFE.

Throughout the rest of 1952, the war was fought along the outpost line – a string of strongpoints several thousand yards to the front of the UN's main battle positions. Outposts consisted of a number of bunkers and interconnecting trenches ringed with barbed wire and mines perched precariously on the top of a barren, rocky hill. As the UN's most forward positions, the outposts acted as patrol bases and early-warning stations. They also served as fortified outworks that controlled key terrain features. As such, they represented the UN's first line of defence and were deemed strategically important by both sides. The outposts were the scenes of some of the most vicious fighting of the war. Small in scale, some of the biggest battles of 1952 revolved around efforts to establish, defend or retake these outposts.

TRIANGLE HILL

On 8 October, UN negotiators walked out of the armistice talks due to their frustration over being unable to reach an

OUTPOSTS

THE OUTPOSTS WERE FORWARD positions ranging up to 4.5km (3 miles) in front of the Main Line of Resistance (MLR), spanning the width of Korea. Outposts commanded high ground from which opposing forces could observe, control and raid the enemy, or that covered ground over which the enemy could pass to assault outposts and the MLR itself. Outposts ranged from squad to company size. Some were constantly manned; others were manned only by day or by night. They were fought over, gained or lost, regained or re-lost, for well over a year, and always at the cost of lives.

Left: Marines threw back 800 screaming, bugle-blowing Chinese in bitter fighting on 'the Hook', a crescent-shaped ridge near the Samichon River. A wounded Marine is given a drink of water by buddies as he lies awaiting evacuation to an aid station, November 1952.

accommodation with the enemy on the prisoner issue. With no hope in sight for a resolution of the conflict, UN commanders felt that some demonstration of UN resolve was in order. On 14 October, Gen. Van Fleet ordered an operation to take Triangle Hill, a mountain 4km (3 miles) north of Kumhwa. Success there and on its neighbour, Sniper Ridge, Van Fleet reckoned, would force the enemy to fall back over 1000m (3280ft) to the next viable defensive position, thereby strengthening UN dominance over the sector and reducing friendly casualties.

Artillery and fighter-bomber sorties began pummelling Triangle Hill, but communist defences proved tougher than expected, and reinforcements had to be funnelled in on more than one occasion. When hostilities subsided several weeks later, two UN infantry divisions had suffered more than 9000 casualties in an ultimately futile attempt to capture Triangle Hill. Estimates of Chinese casualties exceeded 19,000 men, but the communists had the manpower for such fights and continued to send forces into the breach to hold key terrain. The United Nations did not have such resources.

The battles for Triangle Hill and Sniper Ridge had wound down in mid-November at the onset of yet another Korean winter. As in the previous winter, the cold had a calming effect on hostilities. Both sides still fired artillery at each other and mounted patrols as a show of force, but no hard fighting took place throughout the winter. Many of the experienced soldiers that had fought in World War II were rotated home towards the end of 1952, leaving only reserves and untested soldiers. As such, the UN relied increasingly on airpower.

EVENTS OF 1953

The spring of 1953 brought many changes that eventually paved the way for the long-awaited armistice. In January, Dwight D. Eisenhower succeeded Harry S. Truman as President of the United States. Eisenhower's presidency created an air of uncertainty among communist leaders. Although he had campaigned on a platform promising to end the war, some communists feared that Eisenhower, a former five-star general in World War II, whose Republican Party contained some militant elements, might seek to end the war by winning it.

In March, Soviet leader Joseph Stalin died, creating a succession struggle inside the Soviet Union. Preoccupied with their own political affairs, Kremlin leaders looked to minimize their involvement in Korea. They certainly were not willing to continue hostilities that might trigger a full-scale war with the US during the period of reconstruction. Shortly after Stalin's death, Soviet officials began to signal a new interest in seeing the Korean conflict put to rest. These sentiments were echoed by Mao, who likewise found that the conflict in Korea was detracting from his ability to address pressing domestic issues inside the newly-formed People's Republic of China.

Below: President-elect Dwight D. Eisenhower fulfilling a campaign promise to visit Korea. Here he is seen eating with the troops.

On 26 April, UN and communist negotiators returned to the truce tent at Panmunjom. This time, communist negotiators expressed a willingness to allow prisoners of war to decide whether or not they wanted to return to their homelands. This key concession opened the door to fruitful negotiations. As a goodwill measure, both sides quickly agreed to an immediate exchange of sick and wounded prisoners. The two parties moved towards discussions with the goal of reaching an actual implementation of a ceasefire and a final, full exchange of prisoners. Communist negotiators, however, despite the waning support from China and the Soviet Union, were determined to seek every possible advantage, and the talks dragged on for months.

In June, South Korean President Syngman Rhee, who opposed any resolution of the conflict that left North Korea in communist hands, jarred negotiators on both sides when he unilaterally released about 25,000 North Korean prisoners who had previously voiced a desire to remain in South Korea after the war. The action was meant to thwart the negotiations, but, to his consternation, it served to keep the negotiators together. His actions had actually helped the North Korean government; it no longer had to explain that its captured prisoners did not want to return home. Willingness to remain at the negotiating table, however, did not bring an end to North Korean hostilities.

Eager to obtain the best possible position at the negotiating tables, communist generals decided to increase the pressure on UN forces. It was not the first time such a move had been undertaken. Both sides preferred to bargain from a position of strength, which partly explained the stalemate that had continued since summer 1951. The latest North Korean offensives, however, served another purpose as well.

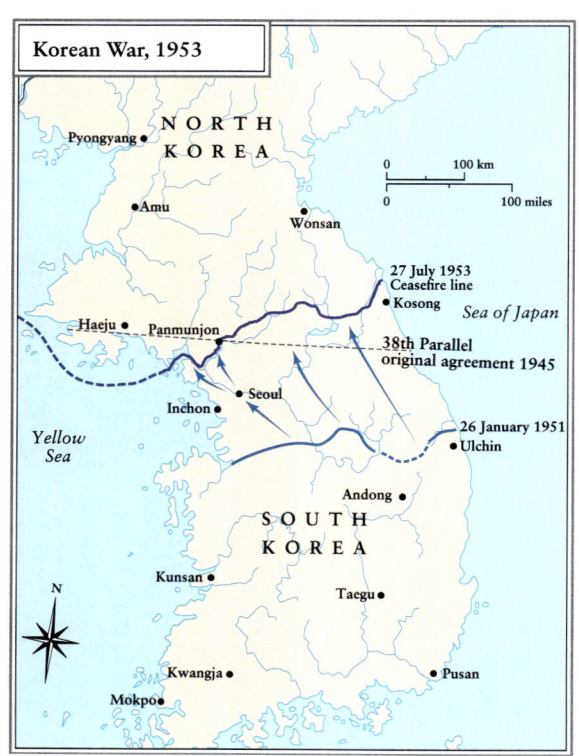

Below: This map shows the ground gained by UN forces between 26 January 1951 (Operation Thunderbolt) and the 27 July 1953 ceasefire line.

A final offensive that seized additional territory would give the communists the opportunity to portray themselves as victors whose martial prowess had finally compelled the United Nations to sue for peace – a feat that could be useful in the propaganda proffered about the struggle between East and West.

Communist military activity had begun in early March with company-size probes of various UN frontline positions. By mid-month, the Chinese had escalated to battalion-size attacks. After a failed attempt to capture a UN hill outpost nicknamed 'Little Gibraltar', the Chinese turned their gaze onto one of the central battlefields of the previous year – Old Baldy. On the evening of 23 March, a Chinese battalion supported by mortar and artillery fire overran a Colombian company on Old Baldy. Repeated efforts by the 7th Infantry Division to regain the mountain failed to dislodge the Chinese. Eventually, Eighth Army commander Maxwell Taylor pulled back his forces, deeming it not worth the losses to retake the hill.

April remained relatively quiet, but communist forces began attacking again in May. In June, as the Panmunjom negotiators sat down to draw up a final ceasefire line, the enemy launched a major, three-division offensive against the ROK II Corps in the vicinity of Kumsong. The Chinese succeeded in pushing the South Koreans back about 5km (3 miles) before the front was stabilized, a significant advance after two years of stagnant trench warfare. UN forces continued to repulse more limited communist attacks until, by the end of June, the intensity of the fighting had once again subsided. The communist forces were far from done, however, and looked to mount another offensive on Pork Chop Hill, the largest one since the spring of 1951.

PORK CHOP HILL

The Battle of Pork Chop Hill comprised a pair of related Korean War infantry battles during April and July of 1953. In the first battle, both the PVA and US infantry assaulted the hill, initially under cover of a moonless night. Each used a heavy preparatory

Below: Soldiers help a wounded comrade after he is hurt at the Battle of Pork Chop Hill, a fight that historians claim had no strategic value for either side.

artillery barrage to force the defenders to take cover in bunkers and to screen the approach of the attacking troops. Once inside the trench line, troops of both forces were forced to eliminate bunkers individually, using hand grenades, explosive charges and occasionally flamethrowers, resulting in heavy casualties to the attackers. For the remainder of May and throughout June, the 7th Division rebuilt its defences on Pork Chop Hill.

On the night of 6 July, using tactics identical to those in the April assault, the PVA again attacked Pork Chop. The hill was now held by Company A of the US 17th Infantry. Company B of the same regiment, in ready reserve behind the adjacent Hill 200, was immediately ordered to assist, but within an hour, Company A reported hand-to-hand combat in the trenches. A major battle was brewing, and division headquarters ordered a third company to move up.

> THE BATTLE WAS FOUGHT IN A PERSISTENT MONSOON RAIN FOR THE FIRST THREE DAYS, MAKING BOTH RESUPPLY AND EVACUATION OF CASUALTIES DIFFICULT.

The battle was fought in a persistent monsoon rain for the first three days, making both resupply and evacuation of casualties difficult. On the second night, the PVA made a new push to take the hill, forcing the 7th Division to again reinforce. Parts of four companies defended Pork Chop under a storm of artillery fire from both sides.

At daybreak on 8 July, the rain temporarily ended, and the initial defenders were withdrawn. A fresh battalion, the 2nd Battalion of the 17th, counter-attacked and re-took the hill, setting up a night defensive perimeter. On both 9 and 10 July, the two sides attacked and counter-attacked. A large part of both PVA divisions were committed to the battle, and ultimately five battalions of the 17th and 32nd Infantry Regiments were engaged, making nine counter-attacks over four days.

On the morning of 11 July, the commander of US I Corps decided to abandon Pork Chop Hill to the PVA, and the 7th Division withdrew under fire. Six Chinese divisions slammed into UN lines south of Kumsong. The ROK II Corps once again bore the brunt of the assault, falling back in confusion for 13km

THE KOREAN ARMISTICE AGREEMENT

THE KOREAN ARMISTICE AGREEMENT brought about a complete cessation of hostilities of the Korean War. It was signed by US Army Lt. Gen. William Harrison, Jr, representing the United Nations Command (UNC); North Korean General Nam Il, representing the Korean People's Army (KPA); and the Chinese People's Volunteer Army (PVA). The armistice was signed on 27 July 1953 and was designed to ensure an end to all acts of armed force in Korea until a final peaceful settlement was achieved.

However, South Korea never signed the Armistice Agreement, due to President Syngman Rhee's refusal to accept the division of Korea, which is why there has still – even to this day – been no declaration confirming the war's end.

Below: 23 July 1953: General W.K. Harrison, Jr (left table) and North Korean General Nam Il (right table), sign an armistice agreement ending the three-year Korean conflict – a feat that took 158 meetings and two years of bitter fighting following the offensive phase of the war to realize.

(8 miles) before regrouping along the banks of the Kumsong River. UN counter-attacks regained some of this lost ground, but there seemed little point in pressing the issue. On 20 July, the negotiators reached an armistice agreement, which they signed seven days later in a ceremony at Panmunjom. At 11pm on 27 July 1953, silence fell across the front. The Korean War was over.

6

AFTER THE ARMISTICE

The common perception is that the Korean War ended in 1953. Even in the United States, that three-year period used to characterize the war has long been forgotten in terms of memory and historical scholarship. The armistice agreement, however, was a ceasefire, not a permanent peace treaty. That means the countries are technically still at war, in a decades-long conflict without hostilities.

A LL PARTIES involved were elated that the bloodshed had ended, but there was no real satisfaction gained from the agreement. Moreover, all leaders involved knew that the failure to reach a permanent peace settlement was bound to present problems in the future.

South Korea did not even sign the armistice, although the nation recently confirmed that it has discussed signing a peace treaty with North Korea. Even so, the parties that signed the armistice did not plan for the conflict to remain unresolved for more than half a century. They planned to reach a permanent peace agreement the following year, at a conference in Geneva. That conference, which addressed a number of other global

Opposite: July 1953: US soldiers celebrate the long-awaited ceasefire.

issues, convened on 26 April 1954. When it came time to set the final terms, however, the leaders could not agree on the best path forward. The idea of the Geneva conference was that there would be a new unified Korean government established after an election, but delegates could not agree on the process of how that would happen. Because of that, the Geneva conference collapsed, and the same situation in Korea has prevailed ever since.

South Korea did not sign the armistice because its president, Syngman Rhee, thought that the US should have done more to extend South Korea's control over the peninsula. Another obstacle was America's refusal to recognize the People's Republic of China as a legitimate government, symbolized by Secretary of State John Foster Dulles' refusal to shake hands with Chinese Premier Zhou Enlai during the Geneva conference.

During the war, the United States and its allies had captured tens of thousands of communist soldiers. Many of those POWs claimed that they had been coerced into fighting for China and North Korea and said they did not want to return to their home countries once they were exchanged. This presented a serious stumbling block to peace negotiations between the parties. North Korea and China insisted that their POWs be repatriated; the United States and South Korea refused on humanitarian grounds. Finally, as the military stalemate dragged on, North Korea and China relented, conceding to American demands to let prisoners of war either return or be granted asylum with their captors as long as a neutral UN commission handled POWs who did not want to return.

> MANY POWS CLAIMED THAT THEY HAD BEEN COERCED INTO FIGHTING FOR CHINA AND NORTH KOREA AND SAID THEY DID NOT WANT TO RETURN TO THEIR HOME COUNTRIES.

RETURNING POWS

The newly empowered Neutral Nations Repatriation Commission, led by India, sprang into action. The first priority was sick and injured POWs: Operation Little Switch began in April 1953. The communists traded 684 United Nations troops for more than 5000 North Koreans, 1000 Chinese and about

NEUTRAL NATIONS REPATRIATION COMMISSION

WHEN THE UNITED NATIONS and the communist forces could not agree on the terms of a prisoner exchange, largely due to the revelation that some of the captured North Korean and Chinese captives did not wish to return home, a Neutral Nations Repatriation Commission (NNRC), comprising India, Poland, Switzerland, Czechoslovakia and Sweden, was set up. India chaired the commission and supported the POWs. POWs refusing to return to their homeland were placed under the care of the NNRC for 120 days. Subsequently, a second and larger exchange of POWs, Operation Big Switch, took place, with most of the POWs being repatriated by September 1953. Its job done, the NNRC was dissolved in February 1954.

Above: Litter cases carrying North Korean POWs are exchanged at the communist receiving centre at Panmunjom during Operation Little Switch.

500 civilians. However, United States officials complained that the communists were construing 'sick and wounded' so narrowly that they had not released the proper number of POWs, and squabbling over how to exchange the prisoners continued.

The next phase was the trade of the much larger number of POWs who were not deemed sick or wounded. By then, the terms of the armistice had mostly been hashed out. On 5 August 1953, Operation Big Switch began. More than 75,000 communist prisoners were returned to North Korea and China, which handed over 12,722 prisoners from the United Nations Command. More than 22,000 communist soldiers decided to seek asylum rather than return to their home countries; 88

defected to India instead. A handful of Americans refused to be repatriated.

This was an ambitious exchange, and not without crises. The main problem came in the form of Syngman Rhee, then-president of South Korea. He did not want the war to end at all without the reunification of Korea, and Rhee threatened to mobilize his own soldiers against their UN allies during prisoner returns.

Another problem was the condition of the POWs, many of whom had been subjected to torture and brainwashing while in communist custody. Then there were the POWs who were not returned at all. About 80,000 South Koreans were in North Korea when a ceasefire ended the war. Most are thought to have been put to work as labourers, 're-educated' and integrated into North Korean society. In 2010, South Korea estimated that 560 were still alive. Their ordeals in repressive North Korea were unknown until a small group of defectors told their stories.

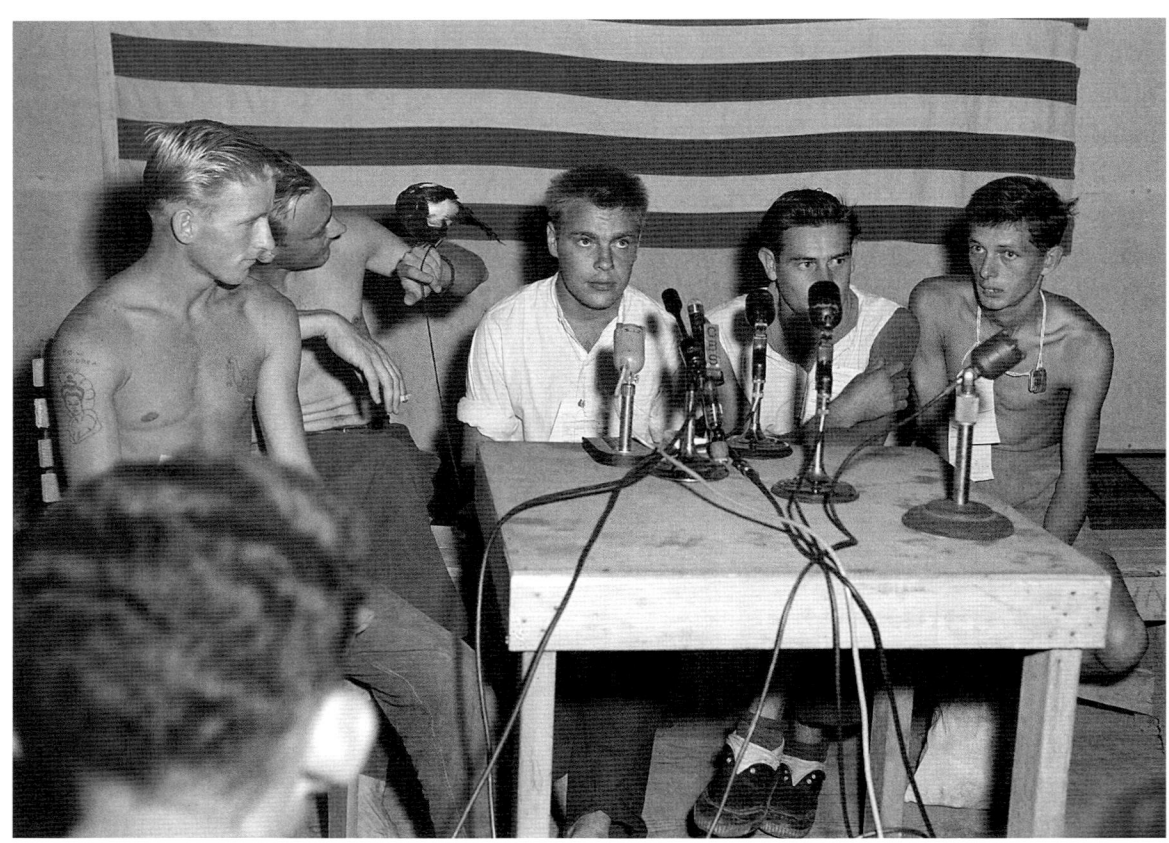

Below: September 1953: American POWs released during Operation Big Switch are interviewed by the press at 'Freedom Village', where UN-repatriated POWs were processed before returning to their homes.

SETTING UP THE DEMILITARIZED ZONE

Although prisoners of war have remained a bone of contention in the postwar era, there remains no more glaring sign of the conflict than the creation of the Demilitarized Zone (DMZ) that separates the two Koreas. Serving as a buffer zone, the DMZ is a border barrier that divides the Korean Peninsula roughly in half. It was created by agreement between North Korea, the People's Republic of China and the United Nations Command in 1953. More than 250km (155 miles) long and 4km (2.5 miles) wide, it separates one of the most heavily militarized borders in the world.

Since its creation, the conflict between North and South Korea, and the United States by association, has been characterized by a secret war aimed at securing the original goal of one Korea. The North Korean government has authorized provocations, including: armed invasion, border violations, infiltration of armed saboteurs and spies, hijacking, terrorism, kidnapping, threats and intimidation against political leaders, media personnel and institutions, incitement aimed at the overthrow of the South Korean government, actions undertaken to impede progress in major negotiations, and tests of ballistic and nuclear weapons (see Fischer, 2007).

While the infiltration of armed agents was originally the most popular form of provocation, terrorism took over in the late 1960s, authorized by North Korean dictator Kim Il-sung. More recent cause for concern has continued under the leadership of his grandson, Kim Jong-un. The first of these provocations was the Blue House Raid in January 1968.

UNIT 124

Park Chung-hee had seized power in South Korea in a 1961 coup. He ruled as a military strongman until his election and inauguration as the president of the Third Republic of South Korea in 1963. Following the 1967 South Korean presidential election and the legislative election, the North Korean leadership

> THERE REMAINS NO MORE GLARING SIGN OF THE CONFLICT THAN THE CREATION OF THE DEMILITARIZED ZONE (DMZ) THAT SEPARATES THE TWO KOREAS.

Overleaf: The Demilitarized Zone (DMZ) fence viewed from Dora Observatory, South Korea. A border barrier that divides the Korean peninsula roughly in half, it separates one of the most heavily militarized borders in the world.

concluded that Park Chung-hee's domestic opposition no longer constituted a serious challenge to his rule.

Between 28 June and 3 July, the Central Committee of the Workers' Party of Korea held an extended plenum at which North Korean leader Kim Il-sung called on the cadres to prepare to give assistance to the struggle of their South Korean brethren. The attack on Park Chung-hee's Blue House (his official residence) took place in the context of the Korean DMZ Conflict (1966–69), which in turn was influenced by the Vietnam War: Kim Il-sung believed that North Korea might become the next target in the war against communism.

Thirty-one men were handpicked from the elite all-officer Unit 124 of the KPA. They were trained to infiltrate South Korea and assassinate the president. They slipped across the DMZ by cutting through the fencing. Once inside enemy territory, the infiltrators traversed the frigid Imjin River and stealthily made their way through the rugged mountains towards the South Korean capital, Seoul. The men chosen for the task were reputed to be among the best the totalitarian regime had to offer. All had been rigorously trained to survive in hostile country; all were masters of combat with small arms and knives as well as their bare hands; and all were fanatically loyal to Kim Il-sung.

Below: Park Chung-hee, leader of a military coup that overthrew the weak Korean Second Republic in 1961, shakes hands with retired General Douglas MacArthur at MacArthur's Waldorf Astoria Tower apartment in New York City, November 1961.

Four teenaged brothers happened to be foraging for kindling on a wooded mountainside some 50km (31 miles) north of Seoul when they stumbled into Unit 124's hidden base camp. Sentries guarding the site quickly fell upon the hapless visitors and brought them at gunpoint to their commander.

RETALIATION FOR THE BLUE HOUSE RAID

THE BLUE HOUSE RAID marked a low point in a period of already bad relations between the two Koreas. Shortly after the attack, South Korea's president ordered his armed forces to retaliate in kind. Accordingly, the Korean Central Intelligence Agency (KCIA) organized its own assassination squad to carry out a strike on the communist leader Kim Il-sung. The team – which, like the North's Unit 124, also comprised 31 members – was dubbed Unit 684. Strangely, recruits were not the military's elite. Instead, mission planners combed the nation's prisons for hardened criminals to carry out the daring raid. The convicts signed on to the risky mission in exchange for pardons. All were subjected to rigorous training on an uninhabited island off South Korea's west coast – so rigorous, in fact, that seven of the volunteers perished during the preparations. It would all be for nothing, however.

Above: Kim Shin Jo, the North Korean commando captured during the 'Blue House Raid' of 1968.

The presence of the brothers threatened to undermine the group's top-secret mission – one that had been planned for two full years. Rather than killing the intruders, the officer in charge of Unit 124 arrived at a bewildering decision: the prisoners would be persuaded of the virtues of communism and set free. The brothers were subjected to an ad hoc field indoctrination lecture, after which all four shrewdly proclaimed themselves converts to their captors' ideology. Once released, the brothers immediately made for the nearest police station to report the bizarre encounter.

South Korean and US forces soon went on alert. Within hours, troops and police units fanned out across the region in search of the invaders. For two days, the men of Unit 124 evaded all pursuers and continued on towards their objective. On the evening of 21 January 1968, they reached the outskirts of the capital. After donning South Korean Army uniforms, the platoon entered the grounds of the presidential palace. Posing as a security detail, the infiltrators passed through a series of security posts, but as they closed to within 90m (300ft) of the target, an alert sentry challenged them. Without warning, the invaders opened fire. Palace guards and police returned the fusillade; within minutes, Unit 124 had been decimated. Government troops pursued the fleeing raiders through the streets of Seoul. A running gun battle ensued. Before the night was over, 92 South Koreans had become casualties, among them nearly two dozen civilians who were on a bus that passed through the crossfire. By the end, 29 of the 31-man Unite 124 team were dead.

> GOVERNMENT TROOPS PURSUED THE FLEEING RAIDERS THROUGH THE STREETS OF SEOUL.

THE *PUEBLO* INCIDENT

On 23 January 1968, North Korean torpedo boats and submarine chasers successfully surrounded and captured the USS *Pueblo*, a Navy intelligence ship patrolling international waters. Of the ship's 83 crew members, one was killed in the attack, while the rest were taken as prisoners. While many opinions abound about the reasons for the attack on the USS *Pueblo*, one of the more prominent ones is domestic terrorism; that it was a way for North Korea to demonstrate its strength and power, and that it had forced the mighty United States to capitulate.

Condemnation of the attack came rapidly from the United Nations and all of America's allies – and, secretly, in the following years, from communist powers including the Soviet Union and China. Although President Lyndon B. Johnson did not want to launch a second war in Asia, he seriously considered military retaliation. In a deployment operation named 'Combat Fox', Johnson sent B-52 bombers and aerial refuelling craft

Above: 23 December 1968: 82 members of the USS *Pueblo* are released after being imprisoned for 11 months for intruding into North Korean waters.

to Okinawa and Guam, 200 F-4 fighter jets to the Korean peninsula, and three nuclear aircraft carriers to the sea between Japan and Korea. Johnson's cabinet impressed upon him the need for caution, however. The US began providing even more domestic assistance to South Korea in return for their continued aid in Vietnam, while also negotiating with North Korea for the release of the 82 men from the *Pueblo*, who were regularly tortured throughout their detention and eventually forced to sign documents admitting to unlawful spying.

FURTHER ASSASSINATION ATTEMPTS

On 15 August 1974, Park Chung-hee was giving a speech at Seoul's National Theatre on the anniversary of his nation's liberation from Japan. Suddenly, a man with a revolver rushed down the aisle, shooting. It was Mun Se-gwang, a North Korean sympathizer born in Japan. Mun missed Park but shot dead his wife, Yuk Young-soo. A high school student was also killed in the exchange of fire between Mun and Park's bodyguard. Park resumed his speech even as his wife was being taken away. Mun, who had travelled to South Korea on a Japanese passport, had been assisted by the North Korean front group in Japan and was hanged several months after the attack.

The incident chilled South Korean–Japanese relations. South Korea blamed both North Korea and Japan, and it took major negotiations with the United States before relations with Japan warmed again. Although Park Chung-hee had evaded death in two major attempts on his life, his luck would eventually run out in 1979, when he was shot at a dinner party. Ironically, he was shot not by a North Korean killer but by the chief of his own intelligence service.

RANGOON BOMBING

While North Korean attempts on Park Chung-hee proved unsuccessful, those failures did not deter North Korea from employing assassination as a mode of terror. On 9 October 1983, President Chun Doo-hwan, the fifth president of South Korea, flew to Rangoon on an official visit to Burma. During the visit he planned to lay a wreath at the Martyrs' Mausoleum to commemorate Aung San, one of the founders of independent Burma, who had been assassinated in 1947.

As some of the president's staff began assembling at the mausoleum, one of three bombs concealed in the roof exploded. The huge blast ripped through the crowd below, killing 21 people and wounding 46 others. Four senior South Korean politicians were killed: Foreign Minister Lee Beom-seok; Minister of Power Resource Suh Sang-chul; Deputy Prime Minister and Minister of Economic Planning Suh Suk Joon; and Minister for Commerce and Industry Kim Dong Whie. President Chun was saved because his car had been delayed in traffic and was only minutes from arriving at the memorial.

Burmese police identified three suspects: a Korean People's Army major and two captains. A police investigation revealed that they had slipped off a ship docked in Rangoon port, and had received explosives in a North Korean diplomatic mission. Suspect Kang Min-chul and another attacker attempted to commit suicide by blowing themselves up with a hand grenade that same day, but survived and were arrested. A third suspect, Zin Bo, went missing, but was hunted down by the Burmese Army. Zin managed to kill three soldiers before being shot dead. Kang Min-chul confessed his mission and links to North Korea, an action by which he was able to avoid a death sentence and instead receive life imprisonment.

KOREAN AIRLINES FLIGHT 858

A little more than four years later, on 29 November 1987, North Korean agents were responsible for an explosion on Korean Airlines Flight 858, en route between Baghdad and Seoul. All 115 passengers and crew members were killed. The explosion was part of a North Korean attack ordered by Kim Jong-il, the

Below: The ruins of the Martyrs' Mausoleum built to commemorate Aung San, one of the founders of independent Burma, after a North Korean attempt to assassinate South Korean President Park Chung-hee.

son of North Korean President Kim Il-sung, who had wanted to disrupt its upcoming 1988 parliamentary elections and frighten international teams from attending the 1988 Summer Olympics in Seoul later that year. Two North Korean agents – Kim Hyon-hui and a man posing as her father – were supplied with a time bomb disguised as a portable Panasonic radio. In Baghdad, Kim activated the timer and boarded Flight 858. She placed the bomb in a shopping bag and stowed it above her seat. She and the other agent exited the plane on its first stopover in Abu Dhabi. Several hours later, the plane blew up over the Andaman Sea.

Upon apprehension, Kim's co-conspirator died after taking cyanide. Kim took cyanide as well, but survived, and was captured by the South Korean authorities. Her interrogators, however, did not harm her. Instead, the authorities took her on a tour of South Korea so she could see the local people's smiling faces and the prosperous way of life that South Koreans enjoyed. Met with the stark differences between the society she was raised in and that in which she found herself, she confessed, implicating North Korean leader Kim Jong-il.

Below: *Chongryon* (The General Association of Korean Residents in Japan) executives speak at a press conference after the South Korean government concluded that Korean Air 858 was bombed by North Korea.

SIGNS OF CHANGE

While incursions across the border continued on both sides, North Korea continued to exist as a totalitarian state, where its citizens were tightly controlled and freedoms remained but a dream. South Korea continued to flourish, becoming a vibrant capitalist economy whose citizens enjoyed a better life and chance of prosperity than their North Korean counterparts.

The first sign of possible change came with UN Resolution 702, which added both North and South Korea to its roster of member nations.

In 1991, the South Korean government had been courting Moscow and Beijing – historically the North's two patrons – to support South Korea's entry to the United Nations. For decades, North Korea fiercely opposed separate membership, saying it would amount to international

TRAINING A TERRORIST

KIM HYON-hui disclosed that she had been travelling undercover for three years preparing for the Flight 858 attack. Kim told investigators that, when she was 16, she had been chosen by the Workers' Party of Korea and trained in a number of languages. Three years later, she was educated at a secret elite espionage school run by the North Korean Army, where she was trained to kill with her hands and feet and to use rifles and grenades. Training at the school involved enduring several years of gruelling physical and psychological conditioning. In 1987, aged 25, Kim was ordered to detonate the bomb aboard Flight 858 to reunify her divided country forever. Kim was later pardoned by then-South Korean President Roh Tae-woo; he claimed that the young Kim was clearly a product of North Korean brainwashing, and that if anyone should be held responsible for the attack it should be the North Korean government.

Right: Kim Hyon-hui enters the South Korean high court, where she will stand trial for the bombing of Korean Air Flight 858.

ratification of the 46-year partition of the Korean Peninsula. It is important to remember here that both governments have claimed to be the one true government of Korea, as evinced by South Korea's refusal to sign the armistice in 1953. North Korea's decision not to block South Korea's application to the UN was announced in a bitterly-worded statement that acknowledged that its hand had been forced.

> As the South Korean authorities insist on their unilateral U.N. membership, 'if we leave this alone important issues related to the interests of the entire Korean nation would be dealt with in a biased manner on the U.N. rostrum,' the statement from the North Korean Foreign Ministry said. 'We cannot let it go that way.'   (New York Times)

1996 GANGNEUNG INCIDENT

On 15 September 1996, a North Korean Sang-O-class submarine landed a three-person special operations reconnaissance team on the east coast of South Korea near Jeongdongjin, 19km (12 miles) southeast of Gangneung, Gangwon-do. Their mission was to spy on the naval installations in the area and then return. The submarine made a failed attempt to collect the team on 16 September and returned the following day. However, the submarine ran aground in the attempt, and all efforts to try to make her free were in vain. The crew then decided to destroy the sensitive equipment in the submarine and try to make it to the DMZ. The crew split up into several groups; one was spotted by a civilian, who alerted the authorities.

A 49-day-long manhunt ensued, from 18 September through 5 November, resulting in the capture or elimination of all of the crew and members of the reconnaissance team except one, who was believed to have made it back to North Korea. Four civilians and 12 South Korean soldiers died, and 27 soldiers were wounded. The infiltrators possessed among their arsenal M16A1 rifles and imitation South Korean-style military uniforms. Some of the dead spies' corpses were displayed to the media.

The submarine was salvaged and towed to a naval base for investigation. Of the 25 North Korean infiltrators, one was captured, 11 were killed by other members for allowing the submarine to run aground, and 13 were killed in firefights with the South Korean Army. North Korea was reluctant to take responsibility, claiming that the submarine had suffered an engine failure and had drifted aground. By 29 December, however, the North issued an official statement expressing 'deep regret' over the submarine incident. In return, the South Korean government returned the cremated remains of the infiltrators to the North via Panmunjom on 30 December.

Continued espionage efforts characterized the relationship between the two nations. Change in the South, however, came in 1997, when Kim Dae-jung, a former political prisoner once sentenced to death under one of the country's early military rulers, was elected South Korea's president. It was the first time in the country that power had shifted from a ruling party president to one from the opposition, and this event firmly established democracy in a country that had spent its early years under a succession of autocratic rulers. Kim was the architect of the 'Sunshine Policy' of engaging communist North Korea, which led to an unprecedented warming of ties between the foes.

The announcement was met with jubilation in Seoul, where officials said it was the first clear sign that North Korea's leadership was changing its policies in response to increasing apprehension about its international isolation. The South Korean government was careful not to appear too enamoured with the change, however. The past between the two nations had soured any South Korean hope that North Korea had turned a new leaf, although Seoul recognized it as a possible stepping stone to forging better relations in Asia.

South Korea also clearly saw the North Korean decision as a result of Kim Il-sung recognizing that the North Korean economy was falling apart, and that he no longer had anyone to turn to. If UN membership represented a major positive development in the relationship between the two Koreas, that relationship continued to be tempered by North Korean operations against its neighbour. One of those incidents was the 1996 landing of North Korean commandos on the South Korean coast (see opposite).

INTER-KOREAN SUMMIT

The culmination of Kim's efforts to improve relations with the North came in June 2000, when he flew to Pyongyang for a historic summit with North Korean leader Kim Jong-il. Kim Jong-il had assumed leadership in North Korea after the death of Kim Il-sung, his father, in 1994. The two leaders adopted a joint peace declaration after the three-day meeting, agreeing to promote independent unification and humanitarian and economic cooperation. The meeting led to a series of reunions of families separated by the 1950–53 Korean War, as well as

Below: Members of the Democratic People's Republic of Korea (North Korea) delegation participate at a general assembly at the United Nations, 17 September 1991.

KIM JONG-IL

Born in Vyatskoye, Russia, Kim Jong-il took over as General Secretary of the Workers' Party of Korea (WPK), WPK Presidium, Chairman of the National Defence Commission of North Korea and the Supreme Commander of the Korean People's Army after his father, Kim Il-sung, died in 1994. Eventually known as the Supreme Leader, Kim was notorious for his repressive regime, human rights violations and growth of the North Korean nuclear weapons programme.

Above: Ethnic Koreans in Japan offer flowers at the altar upon the death of Kim Jong-il in 2011. He was the second communist leader of North Korea.

the launch of a joint factory park in the North's border town of Kaesong in 2004. Kim Jong-il travelled to Beijing to meet then-Chinese president Jiang Zemin before the summit. The North and the United States were also holding a series of high-level talks on Pyongyang's nuclear and missile programmes.

Kim Dae-jung won a Nobel Peace Prize for his Sunshine Policy of engagement with the North. However, this first summit was later mired in controversy, when rumours emerged that the South Korean government had paid the North Koreans to attend. It is also important to remember that both governments had to placate the UN, the US, China and Japan.

Further tension was to follow on January 2002, when then-US president George Bush made his State of the Union address, later dubbed his 'Axis of Evil' speech. The majority of the speech informed the union on the four-month period following the attacks on 11 September 2001 and the subsequent actions to pursue the perpetrators. The speech – more a call to fund the US government's war on terror – clearly linked North Korea with Iran and Iraq.

NORTH KOREA'S NUCLEAR CAPABILITY

In February 2005, North Korea claimed to have built nuclear weapons. A year later, it test-fired medium- and long-range missiles. Development of such technology only served to spread concern around the globe. While the US feared the emergence of another nuclear power with what they deemed an unstable leadership, a very real threat existed for China, Japan and especially South Korea. The test ushered in an era where the pursuit and possible use of nuclear weapons formed the most glaring example of North Korean provocation in the ongoing struggle since the two Koreas had been created.

North Korea had been suspected of maintaining a clandestine nuclear weapons development programme since the early 1980s, when it constructed a plutonium-producing Magnox nuclear reactor at Yongbyon. Various diplomatic means had been used by the international community to attempt to limit North Korea's nuclear work to peaceful and scientific means and encourage North Korea to participate in international treaties.

In 1994, the United States and North Korea signed the 'Agreed Framework', whereby North Korea agreed to freeze its graphite-moderated reactor programme in exchange for fuel, moves towards normalization of political and economic relations, and the construction of two modern nuclear power plants

Below: Kim Dae-jung (left) and North Korean leader Kim Jong-il holding hands ahead of the signing of a joint declaration at their summit in Pyongyang, June 2000.

North Korea withdrew from the Nuclear Non-Proliferation Treaty in 2003 after not receiving the light-water reactors promised by the United States.

powered by light-water reactors. Eventually, North Korea's existing nuclear facilities were to be dismantled, and the spent reactor fuel taken out of the country. All of this was facilitated by the inclusion of North Korea as a member nation in the UN.

In 2002, rumours circulated that North Korea was pursuing both uranium enrichment technology and plutonium reprocessing technologies in defiance of the Agreed Framework. North Korea reportedly told American diplomats in private that they were in possession of nuclear weapons, citing American failures to uphold their own end of the Agreed Framework as a motivating force. In late 2002 and early 2003, North Korea ejected International Atomic Energy Agency inspectors. As late as the end of 2003, North Korea claimed that it would freeze its nuclear programme in exchange for American concessions – in particular a non-aggression treaty – but a final agreement was not reached, and

Right: Dr. Siegfried Hecker testifies before the US Senate Foreign Relations Committee in 2004. Hecker was a member of an unofficial US delegation that visited the Yongbyon research complex earlier that year.

talks continued to fall through. North Korea withdrew from the Nuclear Non-Proliferation Treaty in 2003 after not receiving the light-water reactors from the United States that were promised in exchange for North Korea not developing its own power plants.

WEAPONS TESTING CLAIMS

In early 2004, former Los Alamos National Laboratory director Siegfried S. Hecker, as part of an unofficial US delegation, was allowed to inspect North Korea's plutonium production facilities. Hecker later testified before the United States Congress that although North Korea seemed to have successfully extracted plutonium from the spent fuel rods, he saw no evidence at the time that they had actually produced a workable weapon. In September 2004, however, North Korean officials announced that they had successfully processed Yongbyon plutonium into a workable nuclear deterrent.

But North Korea had not conducted a successful test of a nuclear device. As such, the extent of its nuclear weapons programme remained ambiguous through 2005 and much of 2006.

Right: Former Los Alamos National Laboratory director Siegfried S. Hecker, as part of an unofficial US delegation, oversee disabling of plutonium production facilities at North Korea's Yongbyon complex, 2004.

Although North Korea conducted numerous missile tests, the question of whether they had actually mastered all aspects of nuclear weapons technology remained unanswered.

On 9 October 2006, North Korea claimed to have successfully conducted a test. The following day, North Korea claimed that it could launch a nuclear missile unless the United States would sit down for face-to-face talks. However, few, if any, military and defence experts believed that the North Koreans possessed the technology to mount a nuclear warhead to a ballistic missile. On 17 October, North Korea denounced UN sanctions over its nuclear test as a declaration of war, and the United States and other nations suspected that North Korea was seeking to conduct a second nuclear test despite international pressure. Clearly, tensions were reaching boiling point, but then Kim Jong-il expressed interest in returning to treaty talks. One can speculate on the change in rhetoric and posturing between the key players, but it is likely that Kim Jong-il understood that he did not possess a viable threat. The low yield of the test had initially raised questions in the international community as to whether it was a nuclear explosion at all.

Below: South Korean soldiers watch a TV news program showing images published in North Korea's *Rodong Sinmun* newspaper showing a ballistic missile believed to have been launched from underwater and watched by Korean leader Kim Jong-un.

On 31 October 2006, North Korea agreed to rejoin six-nation disarmament talks. On 2–4 October 2007, a second summit between North and South Korea took place in Pyongyang. Roh Moo-hyun, a liberal South Korean president who carried on with Kim Dae-jung's engagement policy, crossed the border to the North to meet Kim Jong-il. The meeting came amid the six-party denuclearization talks between the United States, China, Japan, Russia and the two Koreas. The six nations were working to implement a framework deal that they had reached in September 2005 under which Pyongyang was to give up its nuclear programme in return for massive economic and energy aid and an end to its diplomatic isolation.

INTERNATIONAL CONDEMNATION

Relations descended to a new low when, on 25 May 2009, North Korea conducted a second nuclear test. Kim Jong-il had walked out of talks aimed at ending North Korea's nuclear programme a month earlier, after the international community had condemned his launching of a satellite as an intercontinental ballistic missile test. The underground nuclear weapon in May, however, was successful and had a yield greater than the earlier test in 2006. The international community nearly universally condemned the test. Following the test, the United Nations Security Council passed Resolution 1874 condemning the test and tightening sanctions on the country. It also authorized UN member states to inspect North Korean cargo and destroy any that might be involved in the nuclear weapons programme.

> IN JUNE 2009, KIM JONG-UN, KIM JUNG-IL'S YOUNGEST SON, WAS ANNOUNCED AS THE INTENDED SUCCESSOR.

In June 2009, Kim Jong-un, Kim Jung-il's youngest son, was announced as the intended successor. Kim Jong-il had suffered multiple strokes and remained out of the public eye, except when necessary to dissuade international rumours of his decline. The international community speculated that the nuclear tests and subsequent missile tests were designed to demonstrate that even in a time of possible weakness, North Korea did not intend to give up its nuclear weapons programme, and that programme would be realized under Kim Jong-un. Two more rounds of North Korean missile tests were conducted the following month. Timed for the United States' Independence Day and coming on the heels of UN Security Council Resolution 1874, the seven short-range missiles launched into the Sea of Japan were meant to be a show of force and direct defiance of the sanctions. Peace, it seemed, would continue to be illusive on the Korean peninsula, and tensions in the greater Asian sphere of influence would remain high. More importantly, the new North Korean president demonstrated quickly that he could be more of a threat than his father and grandfather had been.

> THE NEW NORTH KOREAN PRESIDENT DEMONSTRATED QUICKLY THAT HE COULD BE MORE OF A THREAT THAN HIS FATHER AND GRANDFATHER HAD BEEN.

THE ASCENT OF KIM JONG-UN

Kim Jong-il remained in power until his death on 17 December 2011. Upon his death, Kim Jong-un assumed the role as supreme leader of North Korea. News of his personality has been less than flattering. He reportedly executed or removed many senior officials that he had inherited from his father's regime.

Among those purged was his own uncle, Jang Song-thaek, who is believed to have played an important role during Kim Jong-il's rule and had been one of Kim Jong-un's top advisors. In February 2017, Kim Jung-un's older half-brother, Kim Jong-nam, died in Malaysia. Although details remained unclear, it was believed that he was poisoned at Kuala Lumpur airport, and multiple suspects were arrested. Kim Jong-nam had been living in exile for many years, during which time he had been a vocal critic of his half-brother's regime.

Under Kim Jong-un, North Korea has continued to develop nuclear weapons, testing bombs in February 2013, January and September 2016, and September 2017, and conducting more than 80 missile tests. Nuclear technology has remained important to Kim Jong-un because of his belief that they offer a guarantee for the survival of his regime. During the 7th Congress of the Workers' Party of Korea in 2016, however, Kim Jong-un stated that North Korea would not use nuclear weapons first unless

NORTH KOREA'S CURRENT LEADER

THE GRANDSON OF KIM Il-sung and third son of Kim Jong-il, Kim Jong-un (b. 1984) took over as the third leader of North Korea in 2011 after the death of his father. Known to have ordered the execution of his uncle, Jang Song-thaek, and widely believed to have ordered the assassination of his half-brother, Kim Jong-nam, Kim controls North Korea with complete impunity. During his tenure as leader, he has been on the UN watchlist for crimes against humanity numerous times and has expanded the North Korean nuclear weapons program beyond even the visions of his father and grandfather. Kim views his nuclear arsenal as vital to deter an attack and ensure the survival of his regime.

Above: South Korean President Moon Jae-in (right) meets with the leader of the Democratic People's Republic of Korea (DPRK) Kim Jong-un in Panmunjom, 2018.

aggressive hostile forces use nuclear weapons to invade North Korea's sovereignty.

CONTINUING REPRESSION

North Korea remains one of the world's most repressive states. In his seventh year in power, Kim Jong-un continues to exercise almost total political control. The government restricts all civil and political liberties, including freedom of expression, assembly, association and religion. It also prohibits all organized political opposition, independent media, civil society and trade unions. The government routinely uses arbitrary arrest and punishment of crimes, torture in custody, and executions to maintain fear and control over the population.

The international community has continued to press the North Korean government to engage with UN human rights

Above: 20 June 2018: North Korean leader Kim Jong-un holding a summit with Chinese President Xi Jinping in Beijing in his first trip outside North Korea since taking power in 2011.

mechanisms and to accept and act on the findings of the 2014 United Nations Commission of Inquiry report on human rights in North Korea, which found the government committed crimes against humanity, including extermination, murder, enslavement, torture, imprisonment, rape and other forms of sexual violence, and forced abortion. On 19 December 2017, the UN General Assembly adopted a resolution without a vote condemning human rights abuses in North Korea. On 23 March 2018, the Human Rights Council adopted without a vote a resolution emphasizing the need for advancing mechanisms to ensure that North Korean officials responsible for crimes against humanity be held to account.

The United States government is still the only government in the world that imposes human rights-related sanctions, including on government entities, on Kim Jong-un, and on several other top officials. In February 2018 at the Pyeongchang Winter Olympics, North Korea engaged in new diplomatic efforts with South Korea, the United States, China, Russia and others. Kim

Jong-un had previously not met with any major world leaders, but between March and September, he met once with US President Donald Trump, three times each with South Korean President Moon Jae-in and Chinese President Xi Jinping, and once with Russian Foreign Minister Sergei Lavrov. Such moves might indicate changing tides in the North Korean position yet again. However, most of the security experts in the Western world have speculated that Kim Jong-un always has an ulterior motive, and harbours no designs to follow through on any moves that limit his power within the Asian sphere.

If any of the world leaders could push for real change in the region, it is China. China is the most influential international actor in North Korea. Most of North Korea's energy supplies come from China and it is the country's largest trading partner. China has the ability to pressure North Korea on human rights, but has declined to do so, including during President Xi Jinping's three meetings with Kim in 2018. The US continues to lead the push against the nuclear threat developing on the Korean Peninsula as a result of China's apathy towards enforcing sanctions on North Korea.

> THE US CONTINUES TO LEAD THE PUSH AGAINST THE NUCLEAR THREAT DEVELOPING ON THE KOREAN PENINSULA.

MEETING WITH PRESIDENT TRUMP

As mentioned above, throughout 2018, the US government under Donald Trump held discussions with Kim Jong-un on denuclearization. North Korea sought to have the sanctions levied against it lifted, while the US maintained that such moves could only be made as a result of real attempts to scrap nuclear weapons. President Trump used Kim's promise to dismantle one missile base to proclaim to the world that a North Korean threat was no longer imminent. Kim, however, continued to develop 16 other bases secretly, leading the international community to ponder the real motives of the North Korean leader.

In September 2018, a third inter-Korean Summit was held in Pyongyang. The agenda was to find a strategy for a breakthrough in its hampered talks with the US and a solution for denuclearization on the Korean Peninsula. There, South Korean President Moon Jae-in and Kim Jong-un signed the Pyongyang Joint Declaration, which called for a military agreement, civilian exchanges and cooperation in many areas, and conditions to denuclearize North Korea.

Moreover, North Korean Defence Minister No Kwang-chol and South Korean Defence Minister Song Young-moo also signed a new Agreement on Reconciliation, Non-Aggression, Exchanges and Cooperation known as the 'Agreement on the Implementation of the Historic Panmunjom Declaration in the Military Domain' to help ensure less military tension between both countries and greater arms control. The agreement called for the removal of landmines, guard posts, weapons and personnel in the joint security area from both sides of the North–South Korean border. The agreement also called for the creation of joint military buffer zones.

DEVELOPMENTS WITH SOUTH KOREA AND THE US

Throughout the remainder of 2018, many of the planned exchanges between the two Korean leaders came to fruition, prompting Chinese Foreign Ministry spokesman Geng Shuang to state that it had produced positive effects in easing military tensions, promoting peace talks and progressing the denuclearization process. Such praise came with the caveat, however, that the US should continue to be involved in regional affairs but refrain from its previous policy of applying maximum pressure on the North Korean government.

> FAILED ARRANGEMENTS BETWEEN THE NORTH KOREAN GOVERNMENT AND THE UNITED STATES CONTINUE TO WIN THE DAY.

On 27–28 February 2019, President Donald Trump and Kim Jong-un met in Hanoi, Vietnam. On the first night of the summit, the White House announced that Trump and Kim would sign a joint agreement the next afternoon. However, this did not come to fruition: the talks were cancelled, and both leaders returned to their respective homes. Again, the US demanded that North Korea completely scrap its nuclear programme and North Korea sought to lift the UN sanctions against them.

AFTER THE ARMISTICE   219

Failed arrangements between the North Korean government and the United States continue to win the day – 66 years after the signing of the Korean War Armistice, there remains no clear end to the hostilities between the major players that became involved in the Korean War to begin with. Although attempts between North Korea and South Korea have apparently been more fruitful than any talks including the United States, technically, there has been no declaration made to end the war.

Thus, the Korean War continues to take shape amid growing issues such as Asian competition over hegemony in the South China Sea, the continued growth of the South Korean economy, and the continuation of a repressive North Korean government that poses a threat to international security through development of its nuclear weapons programme and by supplying other countries throughout the world known to harbour groups deemed to be terrorist organizations.

Above: February 2019: US President Donald Trump and Kim Jong-un meet in a second summit hosted in Vietnam's capital city Hanoi to discuss nuclear weapons and the removal of sanctions.

KOREAN WAR: NUMBER OF MILITARY PERSONNEL DEPLOYED BY COUNTRY, 1950–53

UNITED NATIONS FORCES
Peak strength for the United Nations Command was 932,964 on 27 July 1953, when the Armistice Agreement was signed.

SOUTH KOREA – 590,911
UNITED STATES – 302,483
AUSTRALIA – 17,000
UNITED KINGDOM – 14,198
THAILAND – 6,326
CANADA – 6,146
TURKEY – 5,453
PHILIPPINES – 1,468
NEW ZEALAND – 1,385
ETHIOPIA – 1,271
GREECE – 1,263
FRANCE – 1,119
COLOMBIA – 1,068
BELGIUM – 900
SOUTH AFRICA – 826
NETHERLANDS – 819
LUXEMBOURG – 44

NORTH KOREAN FORCES

NORTH KOREAN PEOPLE'S ARMY (NKPA) – 220,000 (mid-1950 estimate)

CHINA (PVA) – Up to 2.2 million (The Chinese People's Volunteer Army (PVA) never numbered more than 900,000 at its peak.)

BIBLIOGRAPHY

Appleman, Roy Edgar. *South to the Naktong, North to the Yalu: June–November 1950.* Washington: Office of the Chief of Military History, Dept. of the Army, 1961.

Ballenger, Lee. *The Outpost War: The U.S. Marines in Korea.* Vol.1, 1952. Washington, D.C.: Brassey's, 2000.

Bussey, Charles M. *Firefight at Yechon: Courage and Racism in the Korean War.* 1991; reprint, Lincoln: University of Nebraska Press, 2002.

Fehrenbach, T. R. *This Kind of War: The Classic Korean War History.* Dulles, Va.: Potomac Books, 2008.

Jager, Sheila Miyoshi. *Brothers at War: The Unending Conflict in Korea.* New York: W. W. Norton, 2013.

Maxwell, Jeremy P. *Brotherhood in Combat: How African Americans found Equality in Korea and Vietnam.* Norman: University of Oklahoma Press, 2018.

Millett, Allan Reed. *Semper Fidelis: The History of the United States Marine Corps.* New York: Macmillan, 1980.

———. *The War for Korea, 1945–1950: A House Burning.* Lawrence: University Press of Kansas, 2005.

———. *The Korean War.* Washington, D.C.: Potomac Books, 2007.

———. *The War for Korea, 1950–1951: They Came from the North.* Lawrence: University Press of Kansas, 2010.

———. "Understanding Is Better Than Remembering: The Korean War, 1945–1954." Manhattan, KS: Kansas State University, 1995.

Westover, John G. *Combat Support in Korea.* Washington, D.C.: Center of Military History, U.S. Army, 1986.

INDEX

Page numbers in **bold** refer to illustration captions

Acheson, Dean 24, 28–9, 126
air pressure 147–9
aircraft bombing (1987) 203–4, **204**, 205
aircraft, North Korean
   Ilyushin Il-10: 141
   Lavochkin LA-7: 141
   MiG-15: 150, 152–3, 154, 155
aircraft, UN forces
   B-26 Invader 80, 144, 148, **149**, 159
   B-29 Superfortress 74, 144, **144**, 146, 155
   Douglas C-47 Dakota 152
   Douglas C-47 Skytrain 152
   Douglas C-54 Skymaster 33
   F-80 Shooting Star 67, 141, 154–5
   F-82 Twin Mustang 144
   F-84 Thunderjet 154–5
   F-86 Sabre **139**, 150, **150**, 151, 152, **152**, 153, 154–5, **155**
   Fairchild C-119: **124**
   Gloster Meteor 151, 154–5
   HRS-1 helicopters 171
   P-51 Mustang 141, 142, **142**, 149–51, 152
   Short Sutherland Flying Boats 149
Almond, Gen. Edward 55, 56–7, **59**, 62, 63, 66, 78, 82, 85, 110, 115, 120
Andong, Battle of (July 1950) 37
armament, Chinese
   Type 88 Hanyang rifles **118**
armament, North Korean
   PPSh-41 submachine guns **25**
armament, UN forces
   4.5-inch (114-mm) rockets **167**
   .30-calibre machine guns 39
   .50-calibre machine guns 39
   75mm (2.95in) recoilless rifles **137**
   81mm (3.18in) mortars **174**
   bazookas 34
   flamethrowers **161**
   M1 .30-calibre rifles **43**, 86
armistice 189, 191, **191**, 192
atomic weapons 10–11, **11**, 155–7
Australian forces 32, 59, 64, 85, **85**, **93**, 93–5, **94**, 96, 130–1, 149–51

B-26 Invader aircraft 80, 144, 148, **149**, 159
B-29 Superfortress aircraft 74, 144, **144**, **146**, 155
Battle Mountain, Battle of (Aug–Sept 1950) 40, 73–4
battles
   Andong (July 1950) 37
   Battle Mountain (Aug–Sept 1950) 40, 73–4
   Bloody Ridge (Aug–Sept 1951) 163–6, **165**

   Changjin (Chosin) Reservoir (Nov 1950) **104**, **106**, 108–11
   Chongchon River (Nov 1950) 105–8
   Chonju (Oct 1950) 94–5
   Heartbreak Ridge (Sept–Oct 1951) 171–8, **172**, **174**, **177**
   Imjin River (April 1951) 129
   Kapyong (April 1951) 85, 130–1
   Kunu-ri (Nov 1950) 97, **97**, 98–101, **100**, 107
   Maryang San, First Battle of (Oct 1951) 130
   Naktong Offensive (Aug–Sept 1950) 40–1, **41**
   Old Baldy (June 1952) 182, **182**
   Osan (5th July 1950) 32–4, **33**, **34**
   Pork Chop Hill (April/July 1953) **187**, 187–9
   Punchbowl (Aug–Sept 1951) 166–71
   Sangju (July 1950) 39
   Soyang River (May 1951) 131–2
   Taejon (July 1950) 35
   Triangle Hill (Oct–Nov 1952) 184–5
   Unsan (Oct–Nov 1950) 92–3
   Wawon (Nov 1950) 98–105
   Wonju (Jan 1951) 114–15
   Yechon (July 1950) 37–9
   Yongdok (July 1950) 36
   Yongju (Oct 1950) 94
   Yultong (April 1951) 129
bazookas 34
Belgian forces 64
Bilgin, Maj. Lutfu 103
Black Tuesday (23 Oct 1951) 153–5
Blakely, SFC Willis 40
Bloody Ridge, Battle of Aug–Sept 1951) 163–6, **165**
Blue House Raid (1968) 195–200
Bradley, Omar 126
Britain
   Cairo Declaration (1943) 8–9
   Potsdam Conference 1945) 10
   Tehran Conference (1943) **8**, 9
   Yalta Conference (1945) 9
British forces 45, 59, 64, 65, **65**, 69, 72, 85, 89, 96, 107, 120, 129, **129**, 131, 149
Burke, Rear Admiral Arleigh A. **162**
Bush, President George 208
Bussey, Charles M. 38–9, 40
Byers, Maj. Gen. Clovis E. 163, 172

Cairo Declaration (1943) 8–9, 21
Canadian forces 59, 64, 65, 85, 130–1, 133, 149, 151, **151**, 153
Carson, Maj. Eugene 39
Centre for the Study of Civil War (CSCW) 157
Centurion tanks **85**
Changjin (Chosin) Reservoir, Battle of (Nov 1950) **104**, **106**, 108–11
Chiang Kai-shek 9, 21

China
   Cairo Declaration (1943) 8–9
   the fall to communism 21, **21**
   the repatriation of POWs 192
Chinese forces 30, 91–111, 115, 118–22, 127–35, 166–71, 175–8, 182, 183, 184–5, 187–9
Chip'yong-ni 119–20, 121
Chistiakov, Col. Gen. Ivan 14
Chongchon River, Battle on the (Nov 1950) 105–8
Chonju, Battle of (Oct 1950) 94–5
Chosin Reservoir, Battle of (Nov 1950) **104**, **106**, 108–11
Chun Doo-hwan, President 202
Church, Gen. 32
Churchill, Prime Minister Winston **8**, 10
civil assistance programs 86
civilian executions 76, **77**
close air support 141–4
Collins, Army Chief of Staff Lawton 29–30, 54, 56, 58
Colombian forces 64
'Combat Fox' (1968) 200–1
Comfort Women 8
Craig, Gen. Edward **78**
Craigie, Maj. Gen. L. C. **162**
CSCW (Centre for the Study of Civil War) 157

Danish forces 64
Dean, Maj. Gen. William 30, 31–2, 34, 35
Demilitarized Zone (DMZ) 38, 195, **195**
Deshazo, Brig. Gen. Thomas 172
Dodd, Brig. Gen. Francis T. 180
Douglas C-47 Dakota aircraft 152
Douglas C-47 Skytrain aircraft 152
Douglas C-54 Skymaster aircraft 33
Dulles, John Foster 192
Dutch forces 59, 64, 70, 115, 131–2

Eisenhower, President Dwight D. 185, **185**
Ethiopian forces 64, **71**

F-80 Shooting Star aircraft 141, 154–5
F-82 Twin Mustang fighters 144
F-84 Thunderjet aircraft 154–5
F-86 Sabre fighters **139**, 150, **150**, 151, 152, **152**, 153, 154–5, **155**
Fairchild C-119 aircraft **124**
Far East Air Forces (FEAF) 140–59
Fieser, Louis 159
forward air controllers (FACs) 142–3
French forces 59, 64, 70, 115, 119, 131–2

Gangneung Incident (1996) 206
Geneva Conference (1954) 191–2
Geneva Convention (1949) 171, 181
Geng Shuang 218
Gloster Meteor aircraft 151, 154–5
Greek forces 64, 70, 149, 152

Hagaru-ri 110, **111**
Hamyung 76, **77**
Harriman, Averell 126
Harrison Jr., Lt. Gen. William 189
Heartbreak Ridge, Battle of (Sept–Oct 1951) 171–8, **172, 174, 177**
Hecker, Siegfried S. 210, **210**
Hill 180, assault on (Feb 1951) 120
Hill, Col. John G. 41
Hirohito, Emperor Michinomiya 12
Ho Hon 14
Hodes, Maj. Gen. Henry I. **162**
Hodge, Lt. Gen. John R. 14
Home-by-Christmas Offensive 105–6
HRS-1 helicopters 171
Huichon 156–7
Hull, Lt. Gen. John E. 11
human rights 215–16
Hungnam 108, 110–11

Ilyushin Il-10 aircraft 141
Imjin River, Battle of (April 1951) 129
Inchon Landings 53–89, **82, 85**
Indian forces 64, 70
Inman, Eugene 107
integration in the US Army 41–3, **42**, 64–5, 70–1
interdiction, US Air Force 144–7
inter-Korean summit (2000) 207–8, **209**
International Peace Research Institute, Oslo (PRIO) 157
Italian forces 70

Jang Song-thaek 214
Japan
 domination in Korea 7–9, 14
 relations with South Korea 202
 sends aid to South Korea 64
 World War II (1939–45) 8–12, **11, 12**
Jiang Zemin 208
Johnson, President Lyndon B. 200–1
Joint Strategic Plans and Operations Group (JSPOG) 53, 56
Joint Training Directive for Air-Ground Operations (JTD) 143
Joy, Vice-Admiral Turner **162**

Kaesong 24, 136, 137
Kang Min-chul 203
Kapaun, Capt. Emil **92**
Kapyong, Battle of (April 1951) 85, 130–1
KATUSA *see* Korean Augmentation To the United States Army (KATUSA)
KCIA (Korean Central Intelligence Agency) 199
Kim Dae-jung, President 206, 208, **209**
Kim Dong Whie 202
Kim Hyon-hui **204**, 205, **205**
Kim Il-sung 15, 17, 19–20, 21, 24–5, 27, 28, 78, **79**, 195, 198, 199, 204, 207, 208
Kim Jong-il 203–4, 207, 208, **208, 209**, 212, 213, 214
Kim Jong-nam 214

Kim Jong-un 195, **212**, 213, 214–19, **215, 216**, 219
Kim Ku 16
Kim Shin Jo **199**
Kimpo Airfield 140
KMAG *see* Korean Military Advisor Group (KMAG)
Kongju 76, **77**
Korean Airline Flight 858, explosion on (1987) 203–4, **204**, 205
Korean Augmentation To the United States Army (KATUSA) 27, 64–5, 69, 71
Korean Central Intelligence Agency (KCIA) 199
Korean Constabulary 16, 22, 29
Korean Liberation Army 16
Korean Military Advisor Group (KMAG) 23, 29, 32
Korean People's Air Force (KPAF) 141
Kunsan 54
Kunu-ri, Battle of (Nov 1950) 97, **97**, 98–101, **100**, 107

Landing Ship Tanks (LSTs) **61**, 108
Lavochkin LA-7 aircraft 141
Lavrov, Sergei 217
Lee Beom-seok 202
Lemay, Curtis 157
Liberation Day (15 August 1945) 14
Loveless, Col. Jay 34
Luxembourg forces 64

M1 .30-calibre rifles **43**, 86
M4 Sherman tanks **93, 121, 168**, 174, 175, 177–8
M24 Chaffee tanks 130
M26 Pershing tanks **41**, 47, 59, **62, 91, 132**
MacArthur, Gen. Douglas 9, 24, 28–9, 30, **31**, 32, 33, **53, 54**, 54–8, **59**, 62, 63, 66, 77–8, 79–80, 83–4, **84**, 86–8, 91, 105, 106, **107**, 111–12, **122**, 123–6, 155–6, 158, **198**
Manchuria 9, 11, 13, 156
Mao Zedong 21, **21, 22**, 131, 185
Marshall, George C. 88, 126
Maryang San, First Battle of (Oct 1951) 130
massacres 76, **77**
McClure, Gen. R. B. 115
McNabb, Charles 109–10
MiG Alley 153–5
MiG-15 aircraft 150, 152–3, **154**, 155
Milburn, Maj. Gen. Frank W. 93
Missouri, USS **12**
Mokpo 76, **77**
Moon Jae in, President **215**, 217
Mount McKinley, USS **59**
Muccio, John 24, 25
Mun Se-gwang 201–2

Naktong Offensive (Aug–Sept 1950) 40–1, **41**
Nam Il, Gen. 189
napalm 159

NATO *see* North Atlantic Treaty Organization (NATO) Neutral Nations Repatriation Commission (NNRC) 192–4
New Zealand forces 59, 64, 85, 130
NKPA *see* North Korean People's Army (NKPA)
No Gun Ri 76
No Kwang-chol 218
North Atlantic Treaty Organization (NATO) 151, 153
North Korean People's Army (NKPA) 94
 Andong (July 1950) 37
 Battle Mountain (Aug–Sept 1950) 40, 73–4
 Battle of Osan (5th July 1950) 34
 Bloody Ridge (Aug–Sept 1951) 163–6
 the Chinese Spring Offensive 128
 Heartbreak Ridge (Sept–Oct 1951) 171–8
 and the Inchon Landings (Sept 1950) 62, 72, 74–5
 invasion of South Korea 23–5, 27, **28**
 Naktong Offensive (Aug–Sept 1950) 40–1
 organization of 21–2
 Punchbowl (Aug–Sept 1951) 166–71
 Pusan Perimeter 46–51
 Sangju (July 1950) 39
 Taejon (July 1950) 35
 the taking of Pyeongtaek 34
 uniform **30**
 Unit 124 195–200
 Unsan (Oct–Nov 1950) 92
 Wawon (Nov 1950) 98
 Wonju (Jan 1951) 15
 Yechon (July 1950) 37–9
 Yongdok (July 1950) 36
Norwegian forces 64, 70
nuclear capability, North Korea 209–15, 217–19
nuclear weapons 10–11, **11**, 155–7

Old Baldy, Battle of (June 1952) 182, **182**
Operation *Big Switch* (Aug 1953) 193–4, **194**
Operation *Chromite* (Sept 1950) 53–89
Operation *Counter* (June 1952) 182
Operation *Killer* (Feb–March 1951) 123, 133
Operation *Little Switch* (April 1953) 192–3
Operation *Piledriver* (May 1951) 135–6
Operation *Pressure Pump* (July 1952) 148
Operation *Ripper* (Feb–March 1951) 121–2, 123, **124**, 130
Operation *Roundup* (Feb 1951) 118–21, **119**
Operation *Rugged* (April 1951) 122, 126, 127
Operation *Strangle* (June–Aug 1952) 146
Operation *Thunderbolt* (Jan–Feb 1951) 116–21, **117**
Osan, Battle of (5th July 1950) 32–4, **33, 34**
outpost battles 182, 183, 187

INDEX

P-51 Mustang aircraft 141, 142, **142**, 149–51, 152
P-80 fighter jets **67**
Paik, Gen. 84
Pak Hon-yong 14
Park Chung-hee, President 195–8, **198**, 201–2, **203**
peace talks 161–2, **162**, 178–80, **179**, 183–4, 186–7, 189
Peng Dehuai, Gen. 127–8
People's Volunteer Army (PVA) *see* Chinese forces
Philippines forces 64, 129
Pierce Jr., Lt. Col. Samuel 38
Pilbong 73
PMAG (Provisional Military Advisory Group) 29
Pork Chop Hill, Battle of (April/July 1953) **187**, 187–9
Potsdam Conference (1945) 10
POWs *see* prisoner exchange; prisoner-of-war camps; prisoners-of-war, North Korean; prisoners-of-war, UN
prisoner exchange 181, 186, 192–4
prisoner-of-war camps 43, **92**, 180, **181**
prisoners-of-war, North Korean **62**, 171, 180–1, **181**, 186, 192–4
prisoners-of-war, UN 76, 86–8, 171, 192–4
Provisional Military Advisory Group (PMAG) 29
psywar 148
Pueblo Incident (1968) 200–1, **201**
Punchbowl, Battle of the (Aug–Sept 1951) 166–71
Pusan Perimeter 39–41, 43–51, **45**, **48**, 85
PVA *see* Chinese forces
Pyongyang 84, 86, **86**, 91, 148, 207, 213, 217–18

Radford, Admiral Arthur William **54**
Rangoon bombing (1983) 202–3, **203**
repatriation of POWs 192–4
Republic of Korea (ROK) Army **7**, **28**, 32, 98
 advance to Unsan 88–9
 Andong (July 1950) 37
 Bloody Ridge (Aug–Sept 1951) 163–4
 the capture of Seoul 63
 Chongchon River (Nov 1950) 105–8
 cross the 38th Parallel 79
 formation and organization of 22–3
 Heartbreak Ridge (Sept–Oct 1951) 177
 Inchon Landings (Sept 1950) 59, 61, **68**, 69, 75–8
 integration into the US Army 70–1
 Naktong Offensive (Aug–Sept 1950) 40–1
 Operation *Piledriver* (May 1951) 135–6
 Operation *Ripper* (Feb–March 1951) 121–2
 Operation *Rugged* (April 1951) 127
 Operation *Thunderbolt* (Jan–Feb 1951) 117–21

Pork Chop Hill (April/July 1953) 188–9
Punchbowl (Aug–Sept 1951) 171
Pusan Perimeter 46, **49**–50
Soyang River (May 1951) 131–2
Unsan (Oct–Nov 1950) 92–3
Wonju (Jan 1951) 115
Yechon (July 1950) 37–9
Yongdok (July 1950) 36
Rhee, President Syngman 15, 17, **17**, 18, **18**, 25, 66, 77, **78**, 78–9, 86, 186, 189, 192, 194
Ridgway, Gen. Matthew B. **17**, 112–13, 115, 118, 120, 121, 122, 126, **126**, 132–4, 136–7, 179
Roh Moo-Hyun, President 213
Roh Tae-woo, President 205
ROK Army *see* Republic of Korea (ROK) Army
Roosevelt, President Franklin D. **8**, 9–10
Roosevelt, President Theodore 7
Rusk, Dean 11
Russia *see* Soviet Union
Russo-Japanese War (1904–05) 7

Sangju, Battle of (July 1950) 39
Seoul 24, 25, 27, 30, **35**, **51**, 60–7, **66**, 122, 127–8, 129–30
Sherman, Admiral Forest 54
Short Sutherland Flying Boats 149
Shtykov, Gen. Terenty F. 21, 27
Sinuiju 86, **156**, 158
Smith, Lt. Col. Charles B. 31–4
Smith, Maj. Gen. Oliver P. 57, 63, 109
Song Shi-Lun 128
South African forces 64, **142**, 149, 151–2
Soviet Union
 air involvement in Korea 153
 invasion of Manchuria 10–11
 occupation of Korea 15, 15–16, 17, 18–19
 Potsdam Conference (1945) 10
 supply of arms to North Korea 25
 Tehran Conference (1943) **8**, 9
 Treaty of Friendship Alliance (1950) 21, **22**
 Yalta Conference (1945) 9
Soyang River, Battle of (May 1951) 131–2
Spanish forces 70
Stalin, Joseph **8**, 9, 10, 11–12, 19, 21, **22**, 27, 153, 185
'Stand or Die' order, US forces 43–5
Stimson, Henry 10
Stratemeyer, Lt. Gen. George E. 142, 143, **143**, 144, 150, 158
Struble, Admiral Arthur 62
Suh Sang-chul 202
Suk Suk Joon 202
Suwon 32, 118
Suwon Airfield **140**, 140–1
Swedish forces 64, 70

T-34 tanks 23, 46, **46**, **48**, 94
Taejon, Battle of (July 1950) 35

tanks, North Korean
 T-34 tanks 23, 46, **46**, **48**, 94
tanks, UN
 Centurion tanks 85
 M4 Sherman tanks **93**, **121**, **168**, 174, 175, 177–8
 M24 Chaffee tanks 130
 M26 Pershing tanks 41, 47, 59, **62**, 91, **132**
Task Force Dog 110
Task Force Drysdale 110
Task Force Kean 47–8
Task Force MacLean 109
Task Force Smith 31–4
Tehran Conference (1943) **8**, 9
terrorism 203–4, **204**, 205
Thai forces 64, 70, 149, 152
Third Geneva Convention (1949) 171, 181
38th Parallel, the 11, 16, 23, 77, **88**, 115, 122, 146
Treaty of Friendship, Alliance and Mutual Assistance (1950) 21, **22**
Triangle Hill, Battle of (Oct–Nov 1952) 184–5
Truman, President Harry 10, 21, 24, 30, **31**, 33, 77, 79–80, 83–4, **84**, 122–3, 126, 156, 181, 185, **219**
Trump, President Donald 217–18
Turkish forces 64, 65, 70, 97–105, **98**, **100**, 117
Turnbull, Capt. J. G. 133
Type 88 Hanyang rifles 118

UN forces **28**, **31**, 64–5
 27th Commonwealth Brigade 80, 85, 88, 93–5, **94**, 96, **96**, 120, 130–1
 Australia 32, 59, 64, 85, **85**, **93**, 93–5, **94**, 96, 130–1, 149–51
 Belgium 64
 Britain 45, 59, 64, 65, **65**, 69, **72**, 85, **89**, **96**, 107, 120, 129, **129**, **131**, 149
 Canada 59, 64, 65, 85, 130–1, 133, 149, 151, **151**, 153
 Colombia 64
 Denmark 64
 Eighth US Army **27**, 29, 30–51, 54, 63, 68–76, **72**, 77, 78, 80, 84, 86–9, 92–3, 96–8, 102, 105–23, 127–30, 131–7, 162–6, 171–8, 182, 183, 184–5, 187–9
 Ethiopia 64, **71**
 France 59, 64, 70, 115, 119, 131–2
 Greece 64, 70, 149, 152
 India 64, 70
 Italy 70
 Luxembourg 64
 Netherlands 59, 64, 70, 115, 131–2
 New Zealand 59, 64, 85, 130
 Norway 64, 70
 Philippines 64, 129
 South Africa 64, **142**, 149, 151–2
 Spain 70
 Sweden 64, 70
 Thailand 64, 70, 149, 152

Turkey 64, 65, 70, 97–105, **98**, **100**, 117
US 1st Cavalry Division **36**, 45–6, 49, 50, 72, 80, **86**, 92–3, 179
US 1st Marine Division 40, 45, 47–8, 49, 59–60, 62–3, 66, **66**, 67, 84, 89, 109–11, **111**, **123**, **134**, 134–5, **161**, 166–71, **167**, **170**
US 1st Provisional Marine Brigade 54
US 5th Marine Division 54, 59, 61–2
US 5th Regimental Combat Team (RCT) 45, 47
US 6th Medium Tank Battalion 92
US 10th Anti-Aircraft Artillery Group 92
US 24th Infantry Division 30–31, 33, 35, 36, 37, 45
US 25th Infantry Division 30, 37, 38, 39, 41, 45, 47, 51, 73, 97, 98, 120, 122, 130,
US 187th Regimental Combat Team (RCT) 88, 118, **124**, 135
US Air Force 45, 75, 80, 86, 140–9, 150, **150**, 151, 154–5, **155**
US National Guard formations 179
US Navy 30, 45, 50, 57–9, 110, 143
US X Corps 54–60, 67, 71, 77, 80–2, 84, 88, 109–11, 119–21, 123, 127
UN Security Council 24, **25**, 27, 30
uniforms
  Chinese **118**
  North Korean People's Army (NKPA) 30

UN **43**, **86**, **94**, 95
United Nations Temporary Commission on Korea (UNCOK) 18
United States
  Cairo Declaration (1943) 8–9, 21
  civilian evacuation from Korea 25
  and North Korea's nuclear capability 209–13, 217–19
  occupation of Korea 15–16, 18
  Potsdam Conference (1945) 10
  and the *Pueblo* Incident (1968) 200–1, **201**
  segregation in 43
  the stalemate war 161
  Tehran Conference (1943) **8**, 9
  war on terror 208
  Yalta Conference (1945) 9
United States Forces in Korea (USFIK) 32
Unsan, Battle of (Oct-Nov 1950) 92–3
US forces *see under* UN forces

Van Fleet, Gen. James A. **126**, 126–7, 132–4, 136–7, 179, 184
Vishinsky, Andrei **22**

Wake Island 83–4, **84**, 126
Walker, Gen. Walton 30, 33, 35, 37, 43, 45, **45**, 46–7, 48, 49, **51**, 68, 69, 74–5, 78, 86, 88–9, 92, 106, **107**, 111–12
Wawon, Battle of (Nov 1950) 98–105

Wen Yuchen, Commander 128–9
Weyland, Maj. Gen. Otto P. 144
Whisner, Maj. William T. **150**
Whitney, Brig. Gen. Courtney **59**
Willoughby, Maj. Gen. Charles 28
Wolmido Island 57, 59
Women's International Democratic Federation (WIDF) 158
Wonju, Battle of (Jan 1951) 114–15
Wonsan 80, **80**, 82–3, 89
Wright, Gen. 82
Wykeham-Barnes, Wing Commander **143**

Xi Jinping **216**, 217

Yalta Conference (1945) 9
Yazici, Gen. 100–1, 102, 103–4
Yechon (July 1950) 37–9
Yo Si-yeong **16**
Yo Un-hyung 14, 15, 16
Yongdok, Battle of (July 1950) 36
Yongju, Battle of (Oct 1950) 94
Young, Maj. Gen. Robert N. 174
Yuk Young-soo 201
Yultong, Battle of (April 1951) 129
Yup, Major Paik Sun **162**

Zhou Enlai **22**, 192

PICTURE CREDITS

Alamy: 17 (Photo 12), 21 (Photo 12), 22 (Peter Horree), 35 (Archive Image), 45, 78 & 79 (Everett Collection), 81 (Pictorial Press), 140 (Everett Collection), 141 (Military Collection), 155 (PF-(aircraft)), 174 (Classicstock), 185, 193, 194 &198 (Everett Collection), 209 & 211 (Newscom/B J Warnick), 215 (Xinhua), 216 (Newscom/B J Warnick), 219 (White House Photo)

Alamy/Granger Historical Picture Archive: 50, 67, 99, 114, 121, 159, 164 and 165, 168

Alcaniz Fresnos, S.A: 47, 130, 175

Amber Books /Art-Tech: 28, 30, 43, 46, 56, 86, 95, 106, 118, 129, 150, 154, 186

Getty Images: 13 (The LIFE Picture Collection/George Silk), 15 (Underwood Archives), 20 (Universal History Archive), 36 (Bettmann), 52 (Picture Post/Bert Hardy), 54 (AFP/Getty), 68 (Picture Post/Bert Hardy), 72/73 (Paul Popper/Popperfoto) 74 (Hulton/Keystone), 75 (Hulton/Deutsch), 77 (Bettmann), 84 (Rolls Press/Popperfoto), 85 (Keystone), 87 (Bettmann), 89 (Popperfoto), 93 (Keystone), 96 (Hulton Archive), 100/101 (Keystone), 104 (Photoguest), 113 (Interim Archives), 119 (US Army), 126 (Corbis/Historical), 128 (Keystone-France), 133 (Hulton Archive), 143 (Keystone), 149 (Hulton Deutsch), 156 (Sovfoto), 160 & 162 (Keystone), 182 (Bettmann), 187 (Authenticated News), 190 & 201 (Bettmann), 203 (Gamma-Rapho/Kurita KAKU), 204 (The Asahi Shimbun), 207 (AFP), 208 (AFP/Jiji Press), 210 (AFP/Stephen Jaffe)

Getty Images/The LIFE Picture Collection/ Carl Mydans: 18, 26, 31, 55, 94, 97, 107

Library of Congress: 8

Rex by Shutterstock: 199 (AP), 205 (AP/Liu Hueng Shing), 212 (AP/Ahn Young-Joon)

Shutterstock: 196/197

US Department of Defense: 145 and 146, 151

US National Archives: 5, 6, 11, 12, 16, 25, 38, 40–42 all, 44, 51, 57–66 all, 71, 82, 88, 90, 103, 108–112 all, 116/117, 122–125, 131, 132, 134–138 all, 163, 166/167, 170, 173, 176–181, 184, 189